Fostering Public-Private Partnership for Innovation in Russia

OECD

ORGANISATION FOR ECONOMIC CO-OPERATION AND DEVELOPMENT

ORGANISATION FOR ECONOMIC CO-OPERATION AND DEVELOPMENT

The OECD is a unique forum where the governments of 30 democracies work together to address the economic, social and environmental challenges of globalisation. The OECD is also at the forefront of efforts to understand and to help governments respond to new developments and concerns, such as corporate governance, the information economy and the challenges of an ageing population. The Organisation provides a setting where governments can compare policy experiences, seek answers to common problems, identify good practice and work to co-ordinate domestic and international policies.

The OECD member countries are: Australia, Austria, Belgium, Canada, the Czech Republic, Denmark, Finland, France, Germany, Greece, Hungary, Iceland, Ireland, Italy, Japan, Korea, Luxembourg, Mexico, the Netherlands, New Zealand, Norway, Poland, Portugal, the Slovak Republic, Spain, Sweden, Switzerland, Turkey, the United Kingdom and the United States. The Commission of the European Communities takes part in the work of the OECD.

OECD Publishing disseminates widely the results of the Organisation's statistics gathering and research on economic, social and environmental issues, as well as the conventions, guidelines and standards agreed by its members.

TABLE OF CONTENTS

INTRODUCTION

This report presents the results of an OECD-Russia co-operation project carried out under the aegis of the OECD Committee for Scientific and Technological Policy. This project was initiated upon a request from Andrey Fursenko, Minister of Education and Science of the Russian Federation, and implemented under the responsibility of an organising committee co-chaired by Boris Simonov, Director-General, Federal Service for Intellectual Property, Patents and Trademarks of the Russian Federation, and Daniel Malkin, Head of the Science and Technology Policy Division of the OECD Directorate for Science, Technology and Industry (DSTI).

The report examines how relations between the science base and industry, and more specifically partnerships between the public and private sectors, can be developed in Russia to:

- Foster innovation throughout the economy in order to strengthen the basis for sustainable long-term growth.
- Improve the international competitiveness of Russian firms.
- Enable the Russian Federation to better respond to domestic demand for high-technology and sophisticated engineering products and systems.

The report draws on the experience of both OECD countries and the Russian Federation in fostering industry/science linkages. It also reflects work done in the OECD on public-private partnerships, national innovation systems and government policies to promote innovation. It builds on previous co-operation between the OECD and the Russian Federation,[1] and the results of a series of interviews with major Russian stakeholders by a group of OECD officials and experts[2] as well as of a special survey of current Russian initiatives in the area of public-private partnerships.[3] It was presented and discussed at a conference held in Moscow in December 2004.[4]

This report was drafted by Jean Guinet of the Science and Technology Policy Division (DSTI, OECD). It has benefited from contributions by John Barber, Juergen Marchat and Hernesniemi Hannu, thanks to a grant by the British Council and support from the governments of Austria and Finland. Natalia Zolotykh (Director, Transtechnology, Russia) and Gang Zhang (Science and Technology Policy Division, DSTI, OECD) provided substantive and organisational support throughout the project.

1. See *Bridging the Innovation Gap in Russia*, OECD Proceedings of the Helsinki Seminar, 2001.
2. The list of persons interviewed can be found in the Appendix.
3. *Public-Private Partnerships for Innovation (Survey of Current Initiatives)*, by Natalia Zolotykh *et al.* The report draws also on information gathered by Irina Dezhina, Institute for the Economy in Transition, Moscow.
4. The conference programme as well as the list of sponsors can be found in Annex 3.

Synopsis of main policy recommendations*

General

- Improve framework conditions for innovation
  - Strengthen the mechanisms for inter-ministerial co-ordination on innovation issues
  - Remove specific regulatory impediments to innovation
  - Remove uncertainties regarding ownership of tangible and intangible assets (*e.g.* intellectual property rights)
  - Define a pro-innovation procurement policy
- Increase the contribution of science and technology policy to innovation
  - Accelerate the restructuring of the public research sector
  - Re-inforce university research
  - Scale up programmes to promote small innovative firms
  - Re-focus PROs on fundamental research through changes in financing mechanisms
  - Secure financing for the maintenance, revamping and development of research infrastructures

More specific

- Foster industry-science relationships through public-private partnerships (P/PPs)
  - Consolidate and expand existing initiatives
    - Prepare new rounds of "Megaprojects", subject to rigorous evaluation of the first round
    - Consider replicating the programme on "Biotechnology for Medicine and Agriculture" in similar (multidisciplinary) technological fields
    - Prepare expansion of the Technology Transfer Centres programme
  - Launch new initiatives
    - Pilot P/PP programme(s) of long-term collaborative research
    - Determine long-term needs for public procurement of technologies and high-technology products that could be fulfilled through P/PPs
    - Help firms develop their R&D and technological competences
    - Build nation-wide networks of actors
    - Support small (public-private) research teams
  - Mobilise additional sources of funding for public support to P/PPs

* This outlines the main policy recommendations which are put forward in more detail in the report.

MAIN FINDINGS AND POLICY RECOMMENDATIONS

From steady to sustainable growth: the innovation imperative

Over the past six years Russia has enjoyed steady economic growth. However, the sustainability of the current growth pattern raises serious concerns. On the supply side, engines of growth are over-concentrated in a handful of industries whose success depends mainly on exports of raw commodities. To achieve long-term sustainable growth at a rate that would allow for a relatively rapid convergence between living standards in Russia and the OECD countries, such dependency on natural resources should be reduced through the diversification of economic activities, with a view to capturing new growth opportunities in knowledge-intensive areas, while providing resource-based industries with advanced technology that would allow for further improvement of their productivity. Boosting innovation should be a central objective of a diversification strategy.

Innovation in Russia: performance, obstacles and opportunities

Russia's innovation performance is strikingly modest compared to what could be expected in light of its accumulated stock of human capital with scientific skills and engineering know-how, and given its overall investment in R&D as well. For example, in 2002 only about 10% of industrial enterprises reported innovations (compared to 50% in the European Union) and Russia's share of world trade in civil science-based products is estimated at only 0.3 to 0.5%, while Russian exports of technologies are ten times less than those of a small country like Austria.

Not only is the overall level of innovation activities low, but with a few exceptions, innovation patterns are biased towards incremental improvements or adaptations of the existing and mostly outdated capital stock and towards non-technological innovation that serves the most dynamic markets at this stage of the growth process (*e.g.* new business models, marketing, design). Consequently, science-based innovation, which is on the rise in most OECD countries due to both active commercialisation strategies of public research organisations (PROs) and strong demand for scientific inputs by industry, remains quite marginal in Russia and is mainly supplypushed (spin-offs from public research institutes or research-intensive state-owned enterprises, as part of their restructuring or liquidation process).

The Russian innovation system comprises solid building blocks[1] and islands of promising developments, but overall, it is not fully functional due to structural imbalances, deficient incentives and adverse framework conditions.

Structural imbalances and weak linkages between actors

- The bulk of R&D is still carried out within (overly) numerous public organisations and financed by the government budget.
- The business sector, including foreign firms, and higher education are both minor actors in R&D.[2]
- Despite considerable downsizing and restructuring over the last decade, the public R&D system remains highly fragmented (in terms of funding and steering mechanisms), with the ensuing risk of "duplication without synergies" (heterogeneous in terms of quality and type of research) rather than diversified according to a sound division of labour); overloaded with developmental activities as opposed to fundamental research or ambitious R&D;[3] and poorly connected to both the education and the market-driven production systems.
- Weak industry-science relationships (ISR) are preventing Russia from making the best use of its considerable human and knowledge capital. ISRs appear to be sporadic, reflecting the lack of absorptive capacity in industry but also the inexperience of the research sector in the transfer of technology and knowledge, and the lack of appropriate institutional frameworks.
- Inter-firm diffusion of knowledge and innovation through networking or markets for technologies is still very insufficient.

---

1. The Russian science base remains relatively strong, despite an ageing body of researchers and stock of equipment. Many world-class poles of excellence in basic research have been preserved.
2. In 2001, business enterprises contributed only 20% of total R&D expenditure. In 2002, universities accounted only for 5.4% of federal funding for R&D.
3. According to official statistics, developmental activities, as opposed to basic and applied research, accounted for more than two-thirds of total federal funding for R&D in 2002.

Deficient incentives and lack of intermediation

- The funding of public research institutes is not provided as part of a systematic policy. The state funding of R&D results from a combination of budgetary channels and programmes whose objectives and priorities are set independently. As a result, the institutes operate opportunistically, seeking funding via contracts from private industry, state enterprises and the rest of the public sector, or from innovation support programmes. Many organisations (and to some extent individuals within organisations) have been entrepreneurial in developing their own "local innovation systems", but these cannot add up to a coherent macro system.
- This is compounded by uncertainties regarding the ownership of tangible and intangible assets (*e.g.* IPR). Such uncertainties complicate collaboration with private firms, inhibit technology transfer, impair the development of spin-off companies into independent and growing businesses, create conflicts of interest for institutes themselves, and may even give rise to conflicting goals between individual researchers and their organisations.
- This also contributes to the underdevelopment of intermediary institutions, including market-based technological services which are independent from both suppliers and users of knowledge.

Adverse framework conditions

- Excessive returns in low-risk/non-innovative activities (due to, for example, the lack of competition or inadequate regulation) together with legal uncertainties (*e.g.* regarding IPRs) that increase transaction costs within the innovation system reduce the incentives of cash-rich firms to invest in innovation.
    - The three basic mechanisms of an efficient dynamic allocation of resources do not function properly in Russia, *i.e.* a corporate governance that ensures forward-looking re-investment of earnings; a financial system that is capable of managing the risks of innovation-related investment; and an active government policy to use part of the economic rents from exports of raw materials to finance investments in the knowledge infrastructure through an ambitious technology and innovation policy.
- A weak banking system, and small and illiquid financial markets.

- Lack of consistency among different policies regarding their impact on innovation (*e.g.* trade policy, labour legislation, procurement policy, tax policy, etc.).
- A grey area (which is still large) between the private and public sectors where actors have a legal status and governance structures which are not the most appropriate to make them either efficient market players or efficient components of the knowledge infrastructure.
- Lack of a clear government commitment and strategy to improve such framework conditions, as part of an explicit and comprehensive technology and innovation policy. There is a striking contrast between official statements regarding the need to initiate a new growth trajectory in order to double GDP, and rather patchy initiatives in the field of S&T policy.

The fact that under such conditions R&D-intensive activities are flourishing in some sectors (*e.g.* the software industry) and that technological upgrading and organisational innovation has been very successful in others (*e.g.* the foodstuffs industry) is an indication that, once certain key requirements are met, Russia has the necessary capabilities, notably in terms of entrepreneurial spirit and highly skilled labour, to position itself favourably in global innovation networks.

Boosting innovation: the role of government

The experience of OECD countries demonstrates that *(1)* the government has a vital role in promoting innovation-driven growth since innovation processes are affected by endemic market and systemic failures which need to be corrected; and *(2)* government promotion of innovation requires the contribution of different policies according to an overall coherent strategy. The Russian government has the additional task of completing the set-up of all the institutions, including legal and incentive frameworks, which make up the innovation systems of mature market economies.

Improving framework conditions for innovation is a continuous, unending process which in most countries often only requires fine tuning and improved co-ordination of policies in areas such as macro-economic management, education, competition, corporate governance, labour markets, energy, banking and financial markets, IPRs, etc. In Russia, the challenge is greater since its transformation into a full-fledged market economy is still underway. It would be beyond the scope of this report to discuss in detail all aspects of this transformation that are important from an innovation perspective. However, four priority actions ought to be highlighted:

- *Strengthen the mechanisms for inter-ministerial co-ordination on innovation issues.* The new Council on Competitiveness and Entrepreneurship may provide an important contribution, if it is entrusted with a substantive agenda that includes a role in defining a clearer national technology and innovation policy strategy,[4] in co-ordinating government support to R&D that involves several ministries, and in checking that broad reforms in other fields are consistent with the national innovation strategy.[5]
- *Remove specific regulatory impediments to innovation.* One example that requires serious consideration is the regulation of domestic energy prices which still artificially increases comparative advantages enjoyed by energy-intensive export sectors to the detriment of knowledge-based activities, and reduces incentives for energy-saving innovations.
- *Remove uncertainties regarding intellectual property rights (IPR).* The draft new law on IPRs derived from publicly funded research, which transfers ownership to the research institutions, is a good initiative which follows international best practices. It should be enforced rapidly.
- *Define a pro-innovation procurement policy.* Despite some recent improvements in the system of state R&D contracts, there are neither clear, agreed principles nor an articulated strategy concerning the role of the public sector as lead user of innovation through civilian procurement policy.

---

4. Russia has employed a variety of instruments in pursuing its technology policy. Such experimentation is entirely appropriate particularly as the design and implementation of innovation policy is, in comparison with most OECD countries, at an early stage. However, there needs to be a framework for monitoring and learning from policy actions. Russia should develop own systematic approach to the *ex ante* appraisal, with concurrent monitoring and *ex post* evaluation of innovation policy instruments and schemes.

5. These include competition policies to increase innovation-driving rivalry but also to facilitate collaborative research; education and training policies to develop the necessary human capital; regulatory reform to lessen administrative burdens and institutional rigidities; financial and fiscal policies to ease the flow of capital to small innovative firms; labour market policies to increase the mobility of personnel and strengthen tacit knowledge flows; communications policies to maximise the dissemination of information and enable the growth of electronic networks; foreign investment and trade policies to strengthen technology diffusion worldwide; and regional policies to improve complementarity between different levels of government initiatives.

The contribution of science and technology policy

Securing conducive framework conditions is a necessary but insufficient condition for boosting innovation. The specific contribution of science and technology policy is vital and central in any innovation strategy. The main objectives, in broad terms, have no reason to be different in Russia than in OECD countries, namely: to support basic and long-term research while ensuring that it is responsive to the evolving needs of the economy and society; to correct market failures which lead business firms to under-invest in R&D and innovation; to provide the infrastructures needed for the diffusion of knowledge and technologies throughout the economy; to promote co-operation among all actors to fill gaps in research capabilities; and to foster innovation in areas of strategic interest.

But the prioritisation and nature of specific actions to achieve such objectives must reflect specific Russian conditions.[6] In this regard, some recent initiatives address the most important issues, but some are still ill-defined or immature and are thus in need of strong political backing for quick finalisation and ambitious implementation, while others should be scaled up and/or complemented by other actions in order to have a more sizeable impact:

- *Restructuring of the public research sector (PROs)* is still lagging, although new initiatives are in the pipeline. An inventory/assessment of PROs belonging to the Russian Federation has been completed, including strategic directions for the streamlining of steering mechanisms, privatisation of some PROs and liquidation of others.
- An important related subject under consideration is *the reinforcement of university research,* and more generally the strengthening of all links between research and education. This would correct a fundamental imbalance in the Russian innovation system.[7]
- An important emphasis is placed on the *promotion of small innovative firms,* including new technology-based firms through project-based support (*e.g.* The Foundation for Assistance to Small Innovative Enter-

6. These conditions are imperfectly known by the government which would require more indicators and information on, *e.g.*, privately financed and performed R&D, spin-offs, patents, licensing, human resource mobility, research consortia, incubators, etc.
7. The OECD has provided evidence that social return was on average greater for university-based research than for research in public laboratories.

prises), often spin-offs from public research (using generic SME support instruments and others, such as Venture Capital or the new Start programme). These programmes are commendable but can have only a relatively small impact on economic structures and national innovation capabilities in the short to medium term. To have greater and quicker impact, they should be scaled up and complemented by initiatives that integrate small and medium-sized enterprises (SMEs) in broader innovative networks comprising larger firms and relevant PROs.

- Regarding the *development of appropriate infrastructures for knowledge and technology diffusion*, an experimental programme has just been launched: six technology transfer centres (TTC) have been created in six regions to promote commercialisation of R&D results created using public funds. However, it is still unclear how such new intermediaries will complement or compete with smaller intermediary structures that have proliferated from bottom-up and uncoordinated initiatives.

Furthermore, there are other needs which should receive greater attention:

- *Refocusing PROs on fundamental long-term research and involving more end users in the financing of public research.* This will hopefully be facilitated by the current restructuring of PROs (as discussed above). However, this selection and consolidation process cannot be achieved suddenly and should be encouraged on a continuous basis for quite a long period through improved funding mechanisms. From this long-term perspective, funding mechanisms should ensure that developmental activities are further reduced (abandoned, taken over by the productive sector, and only pursued with government support in areas of strictly defined national interest), that applied research is only pursued when there are clear public or private end users ready to co-finance, and that basic and long-term research is supported subject to strict conditions regarding quality, critical mass, and links with education. Overall, this would entail increasing the share of both institutional funding and truly competitive funding, to the detriment of other streams of project-based funding.

- *Research infrastructure should be maintained, and often revamped and developed in promising areas.* Financing should not suffer from changes in the approach to research funding. Here Russia could implement proven international good practices (*e.g.* establishing special funds with the participation of the major project-funding bodies, or making project-funding bodies bear the full costs of research carried out by PROs).

- *Concentration of resources in selected research fields* that are linked to the most pressing social and economic needs. This could involve the creation of multidisciplinary research centres or networks that serve both to concentrate expertise in particular fields and to foster research at the nexus of several disciplines.

Fostering industry-science relationships (ISRs) through public-private partnerships (P/PPs): a priority task

In all countries ISRs are increasingly important for a number of reasons:

- Science-based technologies such as electronics, pharmacology, biotechnology and nanotechnology have moved to the forefront of innovation.
- The rise of computer-aided design and computer-aided manufacture has resulted in a move away from craft-based technology to technology based on more formal bodies of knowledge in many engineering sectors.
- The horizontal spread of science-based technologies such as new materials, new coatings and adhesives, advanced analytical and measurement methods, catalysts based on nanoscience extend to many traditional industrial sectors.
- Individual products and processes are incorporating an increasing range of technologies and even the largest firms are having to source technological knowledge and research from outside.

Science contributes more regularly and more directly to industrial innovation today than in the past. The changing nature of scientific research makes earlier distinctions between basic and applied research less clear and less policy-relevant. An effective interface between innovation and science systems is therefore more necessary than ever to reap broad economic and social benefits from public and private investments in research and to ensure the vitality and quality of the science system itself.

In Russia, there are additional reasons to focus on the improvement of ISRs since this would trigger other desirable changes in the research and productive systems, such as increased propensity of firms to invest in R&D, competitive selection of high-quality fundamental research with economic relevance, concentration of resources in selected fields of strategic importance for the economy and society, and consolidation of the R&D system through improved collaboration between institutes with complementary capabilities.

There are many channels of ISRs (informal contacts, spin-offs, mobility of researchers, collaborative research, licensing, contact research) and several ways for government to strengthen each of them. As other countries, Russia must devise its own overall coherent strategy to increase the intensity and quality of ISRs by combining different policy tools: regulatory reform (*e.g.* facilitate the possibility for public researchers to work with or in industry) institutional building (*e.g.* technology licensing offices in PROs) or financial incentives (stimuli for co-operation with business and support to spin-off formation).

However, given the currently very low ISR intensity in Russia, their geographical rather than sectoral polarisation and the disproportionate importance of informal channels, the priority should be to introduce measures that address the weakest part of ISR, collaborative research, and have a catalytic effect in promoting the balanced development of all other ISR channels and associated positive changes in the innovation system.

Public-private partnerships (P/PPs) are the best catalytic measures that could be envisaged, based on OECD countries' experience.[8] They take a variety of different forms and can be used to address a number of different policy issues,[9] but their major contribution is in supporting collaboration between private firms and universities and PROs to undertake R&D.

8. They represent a growing and already sizeable share of total national S&T budgets (*e.g.* more than 6% in the Netherlands) and often now the bulk of competitive funding for technological development (*e.g.* almost 80% of competitive grants financed through the Funds for Technological Research of the French Ministry of Research).

9. Funding early-stage technology development; providing a means by which universities, PROs and private research contractors can be funded to help companies (usually SMEs) upgrade their technological competences; fostering the development of technical standards needed for innovation-friendly regulation; enhancing the capacity for innovation and economic competitiveness of individual regions or local areas and the development of high-technology geographical clusters; enabling innovation in goods and services purchased by public sector bodies and promoting the development of technologies, products and services to meet the needs of the public sector and social needs more generally.

Promoting P/PPs: recommendations

P/PPs are not unknown in Russia but their number, size, technological scope and geographical spread are very limited. This is due in large part to the lack of industry motivation, but also reflects to some extent misunderstandings (or false expectations) as to what P/PPs are about. They are too often seen as a mere financing instrument with which actors could attract additional funding without altering their research agenda. There is thus room for both improvement of existing schemes and new initiatives that would contribute more decisively to increase the breadth, depth and economic relevance of the national R&D portfolio.

Consolidating and expanding existing initiatives

The existing three main Russian P/PPs (Megaprojects, Biotechnology for Medicine and Agriculture, Technology Transfer Centres) are rather recent and experimental but do show promise.

- There would seem to be scope for further rounds of *Megaprojects*. Only when the quality of applications begins to fall will the scheme have come to its natural conclusion. However, continuous monitoring of the progress of projects is vital to make sure that they are achieving their objectives. One problem which will need to be dealt with is how to treat enterprises which are involved in applications in two or more successive rounds.[10]
- The inter-ministerial programme *"Biotechnology for Medicine and Agriculture"* is concerned with a cluster of technologies in the early stages of their development and where SMEs and start-up firms are playing a major role in every major country. It therefore bypasses to a significant extent the problems of the more established areas of Russian industry. This type of programme could be repeated in similar technologies, *e.g.* nanotechnology, or as a follow-on programme to support the next stage of developments in biotechnology.
- The six *Technology Transfer Centres* (TTCs) are a pilot. If this proves successful, the programme should be rolled out on a much greater scale with a much greater number of centres attempting to cover the whole

10. Some of them will be the firms which are most keen to increase their competitiveness and innovation performance, others may simply be opportunistic firms which have learned quicker than others how to take advantage of new forms of government support.

country. Similar centres that have been created as a result of local and other bottom-up initiatives should be eligible to apply.

New initiatives

Another aim should be to create types of P/PPs not yet deployed in Russia, following a two-tier approach. The first objective should be to better exploit the potential for full-fledged P/PPs in selected research areas through pilot programme(s) and preparatory work:

- *Programmes of long-term collaborative research* conducted jointly by enterprises and PROs. The scope for doing this will increase with the technological/innovation capacity and competitiveness of Russian industry. If large Russian firms can build up significant competitive positions in international high-technology markets then they will naturally develop the same need to access advanced knowledge as their counterparts in the United States, Western Europe and Asia. Some private and state-owned enterprises are probably already in this situation. A pilot programme, following a proven model (Box 1), could be launched in the relevant technological areas. If successful, it could be replicated in others and exert a demonstration effect throughout the innovation system.
- *Pro-innovation public procurement.* As part of an overall national technology strategy, Russian government departments and agencies should first aim to build up a picture of their long-term needs for technologies and high-technology products. They should then aim to research these technologies in co-operation with potential suppliers and PROs. Where feasible, this should be done by putting out research projects to competitive tender from industry-science partnerships.[11]

The second objective, to be pursued simultaneously, would be to lay the groundwork for any future P/PP to build on established contacts and exist with or without government intervention. This could be achieved by helping (public and private) enterprises build their technological and R&D competence. This would help improve networking between institutes and enterprises which could be further encouraged through three types of complementary initiatives.

11. This kind of approach accounts for the bulk of public support for technology development in the United States.

Box 1. **Designing a P/PP programme to foster collaborative research: A template**

Objectives

To provide a stable and stimulating institutional framework for co-operation between a number of PROs and industrial firms on R&D projects that are of strategic importance for partners and the Russian economy.

Launch

The government defines terms of reference (regarding the minimum number and identity of partners, their research field and agenda and their readiness to commit the necessary level of resources), states the form, conditions and duration of its support (between four to seven years in order to allow for ambitious R&D), and invites consortia (of firms and PROs) to submit proposals in the form of "business plans", together with the credentials of would-be participants. Compared to Megaprojects, the research programmes would be more broadly defined, since the detailed research agenda should be left to the decision of the partners themselves.

There are two main variants: (1) *the government does not express any preference regarding technological fields; and* (2) *the government selects specific technological areas as the only ones eligible for support. This second option would be preferable for Russia at this stage. This would require that a governmental commission, in consultation with representatives of PROs and industry, determine the area(s) where there is the greater chance to find competent and motivated participants, especially on the industry side, and where enhanced innovation would yield significant benefits for the Russian economy* (e.g. *new materials, optoelectronics, advanced polymers, software and multimedia, etc.)*

Eligible participants

Private (large and small) firms, state-owned industrial firms, research institutes, and universities. Subsidiaries of foreign firms should be allowed and even encouraged to participate. A candidate consortium should comprise a minimum number of firms and at least one institute and one university. A possibility to be considered is to include geographical breadth of consortia among selection criteria.

Selection process

This should be a transparent competitive process, with clear criteria and impartial referees. The scientific quality of proposals would be assessed through an independent peer review. Peers (around six per proposal), including foreigners, could be selected by a joint panel of the Academy of Sciences and the top universities in the field. Preferably, the economic and organisational dimensions should be assessed by a consultant company with an international experience. The final decision, based on this dual evaluation, would be taken by the Ministry of Science and Education.

Box 1. **Designing a P/PP programme to foster collaborative research: A template** *(continued)*

Organisation/management

There are two basic models: virtual institutes with a lean organisation at the core and research being done at the participating PROs and firms; co-operative research labs where most activities occur at a central location. Each has advantages and disadvantages and government should impose only minimal requirements. The choice should be made on a case by case basis, depending on the technological area and capabilities of actors.

Co-operative research centres or networks should be more than ad-hoc contractual arrangements and have an institutional identity (*e.g.* legal status of foundations) and their governing board (with industry holding if possible a majority of votes in order to ensure its commitment and avoid a drift towards research with no end-users) should enjoy a large autonomy in determining their detailed research plans.

Financing

The basic principle is a tri-partite arrangement with resources (in cash or in kind) coming from three sources: government budget, industry and PROs. There are different formulas, but as a rule, government subsidy should not exceed 50% and industry contribution should represent at least 20%.

IPRs

A key requirement is that all participants could have the authority to negotiate IPRs. Pending definitive decisions regarding the draft Law on IPRs, the solution implemented in the case of Megaprojects would be practical. Whereas government could provide broad guidelines, detailed agreements should be left to participants. But the existence of a clear and firm agreement among participants should be made a condition of eligibility in the selection process.

Monitoring and evaluation

A representative from the Ministry of Education and Science would be part of the governing board of each P/PP. In addition, annual reports on activities would be mandatory. A mid-term light evaluation (after 2-3 years) would check progress in achieving stated goals. A full-fledged evaluation would be carried out after 4-7 years. Depending on the results, public support could be renewed for another term, reduced or removed. In the latter case, the co-operative venture would close or become self-sustained. Self-sustainability should be an important objective in the Russian context since one major objective of P/PP is to increase R&D capabilities of businesses. However, there should be some degree of flexibility in that some pre-competitive research in important areas could deserve permanent public support.

- *Building up the competence of state (and private) enterprises.* Companies should consider to what extent the existing breadth and depth of their knowledge base can be maintained. They should identify those areas where, with the help of RAS institutes and/or universities, they can maintain their technology at the leading edge; other areas should be abandoned. Each state-owned company could be asked to draw up a strategy for developing its technological competences including a full description of the external links which it proposes to exploit. This would include joint research projects with RAS institutes/Russian universities as well as a plausible business plan for exploitation (which could involve partnerships with foreign companies). Subject to independent appraisal, such plans should attract government support according to clearly defined rules. This might take the form of direct grants to the company, tax relief or support for research at partner institutes. Such strategies might be voluntary for private companies but if they pass the same appraisal test they should be eligible for the same government support. If companies lack the ability to draw up such strategies, external help could be made available (consultants, higher education institutions, etc).
- *Developing networks of actors.* One option would be to introduce something similar to the Austrian MAP programme to build up national networks based on self-defined structures and thus breaking out of the established pattern of personal, corporate and local relationships (Box 2). Such a programme would bring together different public (policy makers, programme managers, agencies, etc.) and private (incubators, trade associations, SMEs, large firms, etc.) bodies so that they can get in contact, co-operate more closely and exchange experience.
- *Small project teams.* There are many areas where industry could be interested in establishing working contacts with public research but cannot yet identify opportunities for full-fledged P/PPs. Project-based support to small teams of researchers from both industry and PROs could be granted on a competitive basis through a P/PP fund co-financed and co-managed by government and industry. As part of a strategy to reinforce university research it could be requested that research teams include at least one university researcher.[12] There are different models for the detailed design of such a programme, the oldest being the IUCs programme of the US National Science Foundation and, among the newest, the Linkage Projects of the National Research Council of Australia.

12. This would complement the rather small support that is currently provided through the "Integration of Science and Higher Education in Russia" programme.

Box 2. **A Russian MAP?**

MAPs (Multi Actor and Multi Measures Programmes) are complex funding programmes addressing not one individual firm or research institution but whole (sub-)systems of innovation (*e.g.* science-industry co-operation, etc.). A MAP networking programme aims to facilitate the exchange of information between a whole range of initiatives, both local and national, involving programme managers, participating organisations and policy makers. Mechanisms include the building of personal contacts, networks, workshops, etc. This facilitates learning and helps to eliminate duplication (for example, similar research projects being carried out separately in two different locations by two different sets of participants).

As a consequence, platforms on which P/PPs might be conducted successfully could "metastasise" following a defined structure as suggested in the three-step model below:

- First, "get to know each other" on a national level by a structured and planed process.
- Second, good practice exchange (national and international levels) and as a consequence, establishment of new good practices ("define your own tools").
- Third, road map or manual; creation of "institutional knowledge" ("define your own solutions and rules").

The relevance to a large country like Russia with an inadequately networked innovation system would seem clear though the scale may need to be closer to that of an EU-wide initiative (*e.g.* the EU MAP-TN international) than that of an individual EU country.

Financing public support to P/PPs

How to finance the expansion of existing promising initiatives and the launch of new ones? This question is difficult to answer without a detailed knowledge of the Russian budget and fiscal policy and without entering fields which are out the scope of this report. However, one can suggest some guiding principles and venture one suggestion. The restructuring/streamlining of PROs and reform of funding mechanisms should provide part of the solution.[13] But relying only on a reallocation of existing budget lines would probably be neither feasible nor desirable. It is important that "new money" be mobilised, for several reasons: the need to reach critical mass in support programmes so that they can make a real difference, to avoid unnecessary conflicts within the research system, and to motivate the actors by rewarding their efforts to contribute to economic development and sending them a strong signal about government commitment to innovation.

One idea to be considered, whose rationale is the transformation of depletable resources into knowledge, is the creation of a special "Fund for Knowledge Infrastructures and Competitiveness" to be endowed by a very small levy on oil and gas exports. Its strategic steering (allocation of funds to different Ministries) could be entrusted to the Council on Competitiveness and Entrepreneurship, while the detailed management (use of funds for specific programmes) could be left to the relevant Ministries (Ministry of Education and Science for P/PPs for research). This would follow the example of some OECD countries that are rich in natural resources, *e.g.* the Netherlands, where the CES/KIS Fund uses proceeds from exports of natural gas to finance projects related to the development of knowledge infrastructures.[14]

13. Russia's ability to promote innovation could prove to be more efficient when it is not forced to spread resources, but to combine them. Closer linkage between policy, science, education and industry (including both SMEs and larger firms) - all of which should be included in these efforts - will prove its worth within a very short time period and may yield substantial economic benefits in the long term.

14. The CES/KIS Fund will provide EUR 800 million in support to P/PPs for the 2003-2010 period, *i.e.* an annual average amounting to half the total budget for P/PPs in 2003. In other words, the CES/KIS Fund provides almost as much in resources as the budget for public support to P/PPs in the Netherlands.

Chapter 1

FROM STEADY TO SUSTAINABLE GROWTH: THE "DIVERSIFICATION THROUGH INNOVATION" IMPERATIVE

"The major economic challenge facing Russia is the achievement of long-term, sustainable growth that would allow for a relatively rapid convergence between living standards in Russia and the OECD economies" (*OECD Economic Survey of the Russian Federation*, 2004). In this regard, an overriding policy objective should be to make Russia's economy less dependent on exports of a limited range of natural resources and capable to better exploit the new growth opportunities brought about by the emergence of a global knowledge-based economy.

There are many aspects of its recent economic achievements for which Russia should be praised,[1] but there are also many reasons to question the sustainability of the current growth trajectory of the Russian economy, however dynamic it may look. Whereas economic growth since the August 1998 financial crisis has consistently exceeded expectations, its rate is still insufficient to meet the stated ambitions[2] and its main drivers can hardly be long-lasting without deep structural changes:

1. The post-crisis recovery has been faster and more sustained than most observers believed possible. Real GDP grew at an average of 6.7% per year during 1999-2003, with positive effects on wages, income and employment. Real disposable income grew by 12% between 1997 and 2003, and real wages by 25%, while unemployment fell from a peak of 13% in 1998 to 9% in 2003. Government policy played a positive role in many respects, *e.g.* a prudent fiscal policy together with significant progress with structural reforms on a broad front (tax, pensions system, new land, labour and customs codes, new laws on joint stock companies and bankruptcy, etc.).
2. To double the GDP in 10 years, a goal set by the Russian President, growth rates will have to be over 7% per annum over this period.

Figure 1.1. **Income, consumption and imports**

Index 2000=100, seasonally adjusted (SA)

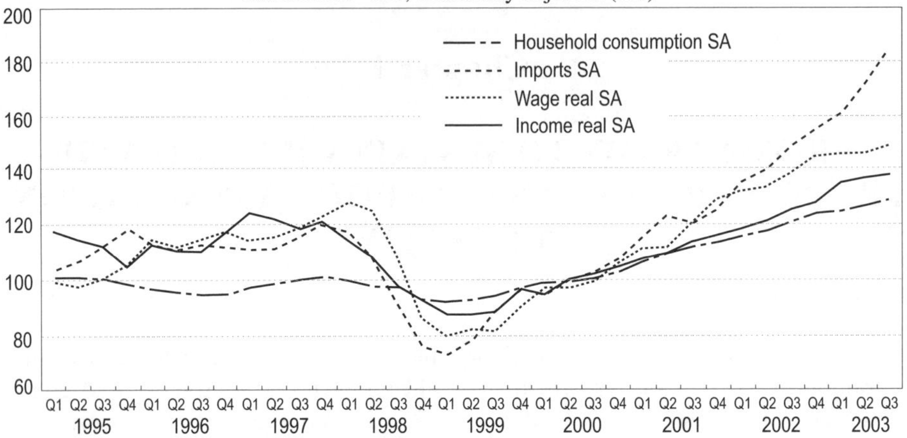

Source: Reproduced from the *OECD Economic Survey of the Russian Federation,* 2004.

- On the demand side, a consumption boom, rather than net exports,[3] due to the combined effect of rising real disposable incomes and exchange rate appreciation. This has boosted imports without putting the external balance of the economy in danger thanks to a surge in the value of oil exports.
- On the supply side, the economy experienced a strong increase in total factor productivity despite low investment rates in most sectors[4] because many enterprises could draw on idle or under-utilised, although often obsolete, capital stock, and could enjoy lower labour and other costs in the wake of the rouble’s devaluation.

Against this, a number of developments point to the fact that the current growth process does not induce by itself all the structural changes necessary to ensure its long-term sustainability:

3. At least from mid-1999.
4. Investment as share of GDP has been around 18%, which is below other catching-up economies in Eastern Europe and Asia, and also well below the OECD average of about 22%.

- While overall economic growth has been progressively broader-based, with the service sector increasing its contribution, particularly in 2002-2003, industrial production has been overwhelmingly driven by resource sectors (Figures 1.3 and 1.4). Engines of growth remain over-concentrated in a handful of industries whose success mainly depends on exports of raw commodities, foremost petroleum products and natural gas. Indeed, decomposition of Russia's growth rates after the 1998 crisis shows that growth rates of 5% or higher have been achieved only at times when oil prices have been rising fast.
- Russia has seen a further deepening of its major comparative advantages and disadvantages between 1997 and 2003 (see Annex 1, Table A1.1). The oil and gas sector has developed faster than the rest of the tradable sector since the second half of 2002. One obvious explanation is the current high demand, hence record-high prices for these commodities. Another is that regulation of domestic energy prices still artificially increases comparative advantages enjoyed by energy-intensive export sectors. Yet another explanation is that too many industries are not competitive due to the still poor price-quality ratio of their products.
- This has led to an increasingly uneven income distribution, which is socially problematic[5] and economically unsound.[6]
- The contribution of FDI to the enhancement of productivity has been disappointingly low, except in a few sectors where branding modernisation strategies allow a quite quick and profitable access to a large domestic market (*e.g.* tobacco, brewing).

5. Quite impressive aggregate growth has not yielded an equally impressive increase in the well-being of the majority of the population. By 2001, salaries of 24% of those employed in industry, and of 81% employed in agriculture, were still below the official subsistence level.
6. Wage differentiation across sectors has not reflected developments in productivity (see Figure A1.1 in Annex 1), largely because of large-scale rent-seeking in the oil and gas sectors. It is particularly striking that gas sector wages, which were already almost four times the average for industry as a whole in 1997, increased at exceptionally high rates between 1997 and 2003, even as labour productivity fell by over 20% during this period while increasing almost everywhere else.

If unabated, the current tendencies will make Russia an even more resource-dependent economy. This bears a number of risks: slighter chances of sustaining the high growth rates that are necessary to catch up with advanced economies; vulnerability to fluctuations in world commodity prices; a danger of real estate and financial bubbles since a massive inflow of petrodollars pushes up prices in the non-tradable sector (the so-called "Dutch disease") and swamps the financial system with liquidity; and an income distribution which is not in line with long-term trends in productivity, to the detriment of knowledge-based activities.[7]

Diversifying Russia's economy is the only way to mitigate such risks by initiating a new growth trajectory. Diversification does not mean weakening the export-oriented natural resource-based sectors, which will remain for a long time key sources of wealth, but increasing the competitiveness and knowledge-intensity of the non-commodity tradable sectors. The diversification agenda is broad but involves some essential tasks: creating a favourable business environment, improving the quality of human capital and business infrastructure, and radically increasing the efficiency of the innovation system. Boosting innovation is probably the single most important objective because it can federate a whole range of policies towards a common strategic goal, and because it requires mobilising what is Russia's most ill-used asset, an important stock of human capital with scientific expertise and engineering know-how.

7. Vladimir Drebentsov, "Diversifying Russia's Economy: Key to Sustainable Growth", unpublished paper.

Figure 1.2. **Decomposing growth**

Percentage growth

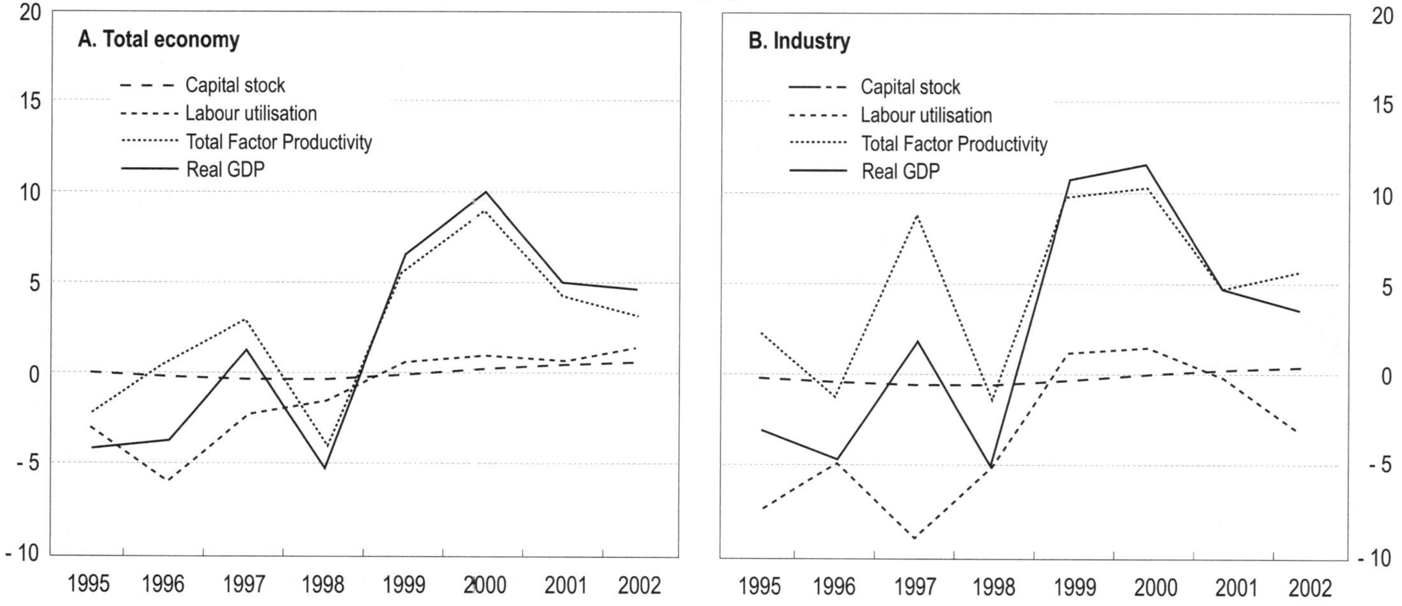

Source: Reproduced from the *OECD Economic Survey of the Russian Federation,* 2004.

Figure 1.3. **Contribution to GDP growth of the main economic activities**

Percentage of GDP in previous period

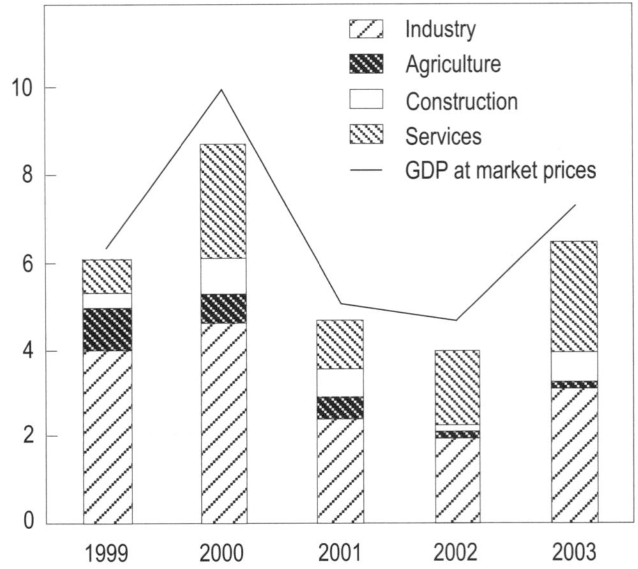

Figure 1.4. **Contribution of resource-related sectors to industrial production growth**

Percentage

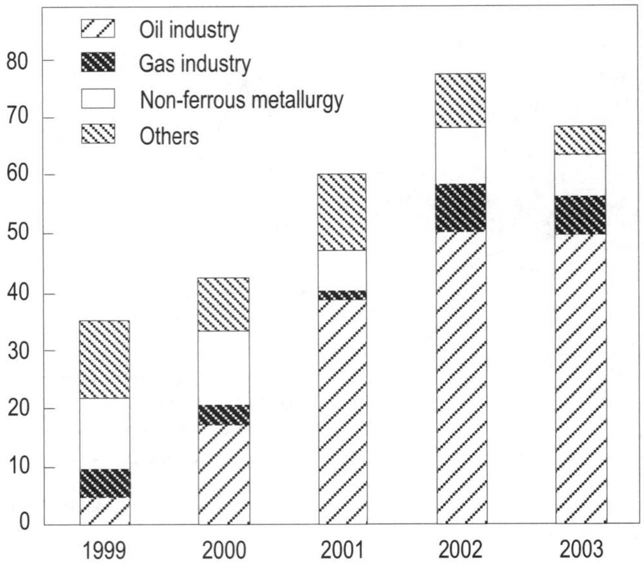

Source: Reproduced from the *OECD Economic Survey of the Russian Federation*, 2004.

Chapter 2

THE RUSSIAN INNOVATION SYSTEM: MAIN FEATURES, STRENGTHS AND WEAKNESSES

Weak innovation performance

Russia's innovation performance remains strikingly modest. In 2002, only slightly more than 10% of industrial enterprises reported innovations (compared to 50% in the European Union) and Russia's share of world trade in civil science-based products is estimated at only 0.3 to 0.5%, while Russian exports of technologies are ten times less than those of a small country like Austria. Another indication is the very low proportion of Russian inventions that are implemented in practice, reflecting not only a mismatch between the orientations of the research system and the needs of the economy, or regulatory obstacles to the commercialisation of research (*e.g.* unclear IPR legislation), but also the lack of innovative end users.[1] A revealing fact is also the exceptionally high dependency of the Russian economy on imports of products, such as investment goods and consumer durables, for which technological innovation is key to international competitiveness.

Not only is their overall level low, but innovation activities generally lack ambition when they concern products and processes or are otherwise mainly linked to the adoption of foreign best management and marketing practices (*e.g.* new business models, marketing, design) in sectors that serve the most dynamic parts of domestic markets at this stage of the growth process (*e.g.* food and beverages, distribution). Technological innovation is primarily aimed at incremental improvements or adaptations of the existing

1. Whereas at the end of the Soviet period about 30% of inventions were implemented in practice, in the early 1990s this ratio fell to 7-8%, and since 1997 it has been below 2%.

and mostly outdated capital stock.[2] Consequently, with a few exceptions, science-based innovation remains marginal in private firms and occurs largely as the by-product of the painful restructuring of the public sector (spin-offs from public research institutes or research-intensive state-owned enterprises, as part of their restructuring or liquidation process). All in all, this explains why the vast majority of innovative firms are not trying to enter foreign markets and thus fail to experience the full stimulus of competition for ingenuity and quality, although there are already bright exceptions, as in the software industry (Box 2.1).

Box 2.1. **Software: a booming export-oriented knowledge-based industry**

Russia is experiencing very rapid growth in software design and development, and related research. This "Russian software development revolution" is comparable to those in India and Israel. The main products are: general-purpose software packages, software packages customized for companies' needs, integrated systems, and information security. Offshore programming plays an important role. The market is dominated by small and medium-sized companies which occupy small market niches, so they do not compete with each other, but with foreign software developers both in the domestic and international markets. The most successful ones are small companies with flexible organisational structures founded on the basis of major universities and research institutions and inheriting their major competitive advantages, as well as R&D centres established in Russia by international ICT corporations (see Box 2.2).

Figure 2.1. **Dynamics of Russian software exports**

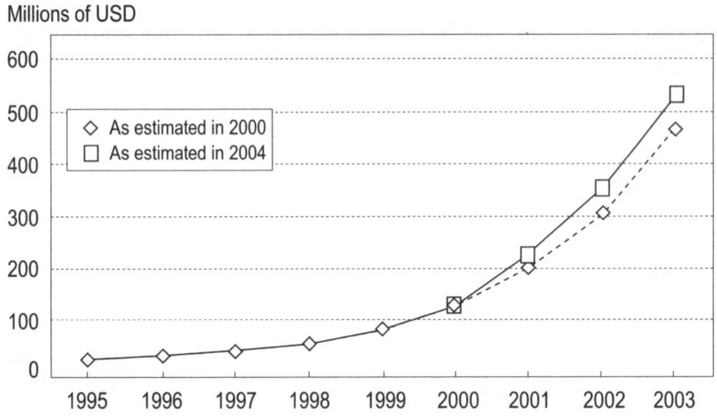

Source: Market Visio/EDC, November 2000; Fort Ross, July 2004.

2. The major share of expenditures on innovation by the Russian enterprises is spent for the acquisition of machinery and other investment goods, including imports of often rather obsolete equipment. In 2002, R&D represented only 13.6% of these innovation expenditures.

Box 2.1. **Software: a booming export-oriented knowledge-based industry** *(continued)*

Figure 2.2. **Main offshore programming centres in Russia**

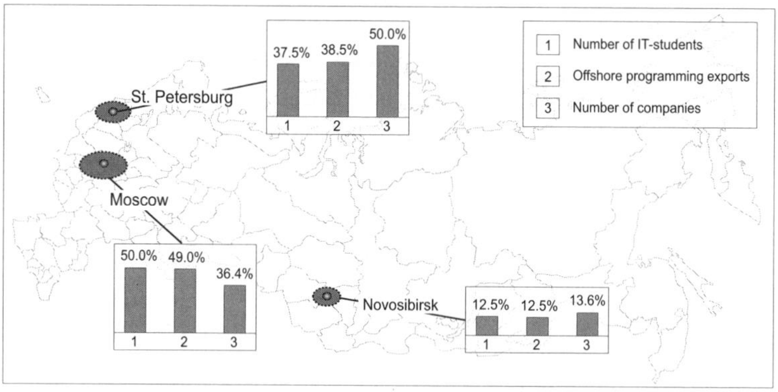

Source: Fort Ross.

Severe inefficiencies within the Russian innovation system (Annex 1, Figure A1.2) explain such disappointing performances. This system comprises solid building blocks and islands of promising developments but, overall, it is not fully functional due to structural imbalances, deficient incentives and adverse framework conditions.

Structural imbalances and weak linkages between actors

After a collapse in the initial stage of the economic transformation, total R&D expenditures of Russia have grown steadily, with an acceleration since 2001 but, as a percentage of GDP, they remain far below those of the majority of OECD countries (Figure 2.3). The bulk of R&D is still carried out within a very large number of public organisations and financed through the government budget (Table 2.2). The institutional complexity of the Russian research system - in terms of legal status, ownership, and funding mechanisms - makes it very difficult to draw a precise quantified picture. The totality of scientific research but also the bulk of industrial research is performed by the public sector in different types of organisations (see Table 2.2): research institutes of the six Academies – especially the Russian

Academy of Sciences (RAS), university laboratories, design bureaus, the research branch of state-owned industrial firms, etc. The dominance of state-owned organisations in the performance of R&D is illustrated in Figure 2.4 (see also Annex 1, Table A1.2).[3]

Figure 2.3. **Evolution of total expenditures on R&D**

Percentage of GDP

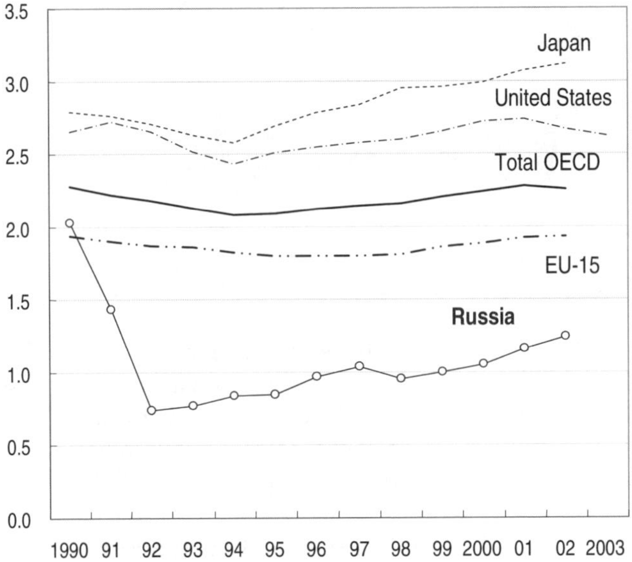

3. The fact that OECD internationally harmonised statistics indicate a relatively high share of R&D performed by the business sector may in fact reflect a statistical illusion. Private enterprises actually account for a rather low share of business R&D, the bulk still being carried out in public or partly public industrial research institutes or design bureaus. See D. Malkin, "*R&D trends in Russia*: *Decline of the S&T System?*" Economic Trends, Helsinki (2001).

Table 2.1. **R&D in Russia**

	2001	2002	2003
Total expenditure on R&D, USD million in current prices	3 607	4 306	5 641
As % of GDP	*1.16*	*1.24*	*1.30*
Government budget expenditure on R&D, USD million	2 029	2 470	3 267
As % of GDP	*0.66*	*0.71*	*0.75*
Total number of researchers	422 176	414 676	409 300
As % of total labour force	*0.6*	*0.6*	*0.6*
o Of which highly qualified researchers*	104 414	102 346	102 451
o *As % of total number of researchers*	*24.8*	*24.6*	*25.1*

* Candidates and doctors in science.
Source: Goskomstat.

Table 2.2. **R&D by funding source and by performer**

Percentage

	1995	1998	2002
GERD by funding source			
Government budget	61.5	53.5	57.4
Non-budget public funds and industry*	33.6	34.9	33.6
Other national sources	0.3	1.2	1.0
Foreign	4.6	10.3	8.0
GERD by performer			
Government institutes**	26.1	25.8	24.5
Other public institutes and industry*	68.5	69.0	69.9
Higher education	5.4	5.2	5.4
Non-profit organisations	0.0	0.1	0.2

* All organisations whose major function is manufacturing, including those that belong to the state; private non-profit organisations that serve industrial enterprises: former branch R&D institutes, design bureaus, experimental stations, development organisations.
** Mainly the research institutes of the Academies.
Source: Comparative Study of National R&D Policy and R&D Data Systems in the United States and Russia, AAAS/NSF, 2001; *Science in Russia at a Glance: 2003*, Statistical Yearbook, 2003.

Table 2.3. **Number and types of organisations conducting R&D in Russia**

	1992	1995	1998	1999	2000	2001	2002
R&D organisations -- Total	4 555	4 059	4 019	4 089	4 099	4 073	3 906
From which:							
Research institutes	2 077	2 284	2 549	2 603	2 686	2 676	2 630
from which academic institutes	*729*	*787*	*775*	*782*	*807*	*819*	*810*
Higher education institutions	446	408	393	387	390	388	390
Design bureaus	865	548	381	360	318	289	257
Development organisations	495	207	108	97	85	81	76
Industrial enterprises	369	348	267	319	317	319	289
Others	303	264	321	323	303	284	264

Source: Science in Russia, Statistical Yearbook, State Committee on Statistics of RF, 2001; *Science in Russia at a Glance: 2003*, Statistical Yearbook, 2003.

Figure 2.4. **Ownership of the Russian R&D sector**

Percentage of the total value of fixed capital, 2002

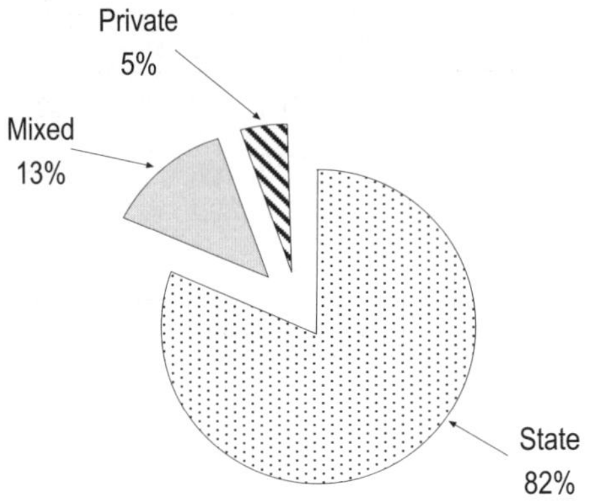

Source: Goskomstat.

Among public organisations, higher education is a very minor actor in R&D. In 2002, universities accounted only for 5.4% of federal funding for R&D. This is a legacy of the Soviet system which has not been corrected, despite the relatively good research performance of university-based laboratories, compared to other research organisations, in terms of both publications and contract research. Until very recently universities did not even receive budgetary support for basic research. Only in 2003 did the federal budget law open a new line to provide such support.

Overall, the Russian science base remains relatively strong, despite an ageing body of researchers and stock of equipment, and brain drain which was particularly severe in the second half of the 1990s. Many world-class poles of excellence in basic research have been preserved. However, despite some downsizing and restructuring over the last decade, the public R&D system remains highly fragmented, with the ensuing risk of "duplication without synergies", heterogeneous (in terms of quality and type of research), rather than diversified according to a sound division of labour, and over-loaded with developmental activities, as opposed to fundamental research or ambitious R&D. In 2002, according to official statistics, developmental activities, as opposed to basic and applied research, accounted for more than two-thirds of total federal funding for R&D.

The Achilles' heel of the Russian innovation system is the weakness of corporate R&D, despite some encouraging developments over the last two to three years.[4] The efforts to transfer near-market research from public organisations to business firms, to promote the creation of technology-based firms, to encourage private investment in R&D, and to attract R&D-intensive foreign investment have not been entirely successful. The reasons are many[5] but the fact is that business enterprises contributed no more than 20% of total R&D expenditure in 2002.[6] In addition, although the empirical evidence is weak, a reasonable guess is that the domestic business sector (private firms as well as state-controlled manufacturing and service enterprises) is mainly involved in the development part of R&D and has a

4. Russian firms seem to show a growing interest in financing R&D and in the creation of their own in-house research facilities. The most active are resource extracting industries. Thus, R&D divisions were opened at TNK, Yukos, Lukoil, Norilsk Nickel, and Systema.

5. Innovation in industry, other than the adoption of best practices from abroad, appears to be low and the capability to undertake it successfully seems not all that strong. Profits, which in OECD countries generate much of the funding for innovation, are also probably low in many sectors.

6. In 2002, 5.6% of industrial enterprises had their own R&D division.

stronger propensity than its Western counterparts to import R&D as embodied in equipment. This has important implications for domestic producers of such equipment, which find it hard to devise and finance a survival strategy through technological upgrading and thus to sustain an ambitious R&D agenda. They were too large, with deterrent liabilities, to attract foreign investors. Apart from liquidation, their only perspective may be to transform themselves into breeding places for new small enterprises that try to match selected parts of their research and technological portfolio with market opportunities (Box 2.4). This process of course entails the loss of quite large portions of such portfolio, unless it is complemented by the privatisation of those lines of business with market potential which are beyond the capabilities of small new firms.

Foreign firms invest according to their global export and outsourcing strategies, considering the comparative advantage of Russia and risk/reward ratios for different types of investment. So far, except in a few areas (*e.g.* ICTs, and oil exploration, see Boxes 2.3 and 2.4), this has generally not led them to establish R&D facilities in Russia or to be very active in creating bridges between Russian science and markets. Foreign-owned firms are probably in the classic MNE mode of using technology developed at home to address the Russian market. Innovation is probably confined to near-market development to adapt such technologies to the particular needs of Russia. They are probably undertaking some more fundamental R&D in areas where Russian science is particularly advanced, but this is mostly cherry-picking with mainly foreign markets in mind.

Box 2.2. **Foreign investment in R&D – the case of ICTs**

Several leading foreign companies in the ICT business have opened research and development (R&D) or dedicated development centres (DDC) in Russia. Russia is increasingly competing with India for software outsourcing projects, though some kind of division of labour may also exist. According to Steve Chase, head of the Russian Intel branch, "Give the urgent projects to the Americans, big projects to the Indians, and the impossible ones to the Russians". There are also some signs that Russian ICT experts who emigrated to the United States and Israel are catalysing the software business in, and even moving their businesses to, Russia.

- Sun Microsystems has three teams of programmers in Moscow, Novosibirsk and St. Petersburg, totalling around 150 experts. In the summer of 2004, the company set up its Engineering Centre in St. Petersburg, with a total of around 150 developers.
- Motorola has the most experienced DDC in Russia so far. Motorola's DDC was established in St. Petersburg in 1995 and now employs up to 350 developers.
- Microsoft employs 150 people, mostly for sales and customer support. A programming team in Moscow produces Microsoft programmes in Russian.
- Intel: The purchase by Intel of two Russian technology companies, Elbrus and UniPro, has increased the number of Intel researchers in Russia from 900 to 1 550 engineers and staff.
- Huawei Technologies: China's largest maker of telecom equipment has opened an R&D centre in Moscow.
- Cadence Design Systems: In 2004, the company opened an electronic design automation (EDA) research and development centre in Moscow which will house more than 70 employees. It also will serve as centre for training, scientific endeavours and large-scale educational programmes, as well as local customer support.
- Metacommunications: This US software development company opened an R&D centre in St. Petersburg in May 2004.
- Boeing: For several years the company has employed a rather large group of developers based in Luxoft, Moscow. Boeing employs a total of 40 workers in Moscow.
- Dell Computers: A very similar job has recently been done for Dell by Luxoft.
- LG Electronics: The company set up a development centre in St. Petersburg in the 1990s, and now employs up to 30 developers there.
- Siemens set up an R&D team in St. Petersburg that concentrates on optical transmission. Around 1 000 people, mostly involved in sales, are employed at Siemens' Russian headquarters in Moscow.
- Togethersoft was one of the first DDCs in Russia at the beginning of the 1990s. In 2003, Borland acquired the whole team operating in St. Petersburg.

Source: TEKES.

Box 2.3. **The contribution of foreign investment to harnessing Russian scientific capabilities to the benefit of the oil and gas industry: The case of Schlumberger**

Schlumberger is a leading company supplying technology, project management and information solutions to the oil and gas industry. It employs over 50 000 people in 100 countries. Its revenue in 2003 was around USD 10 billion. The company has been present in Russia since 1929, selling products and services to Russian industry. In recent years it has taken new initiatives to involve the Russian scientific community in its R&D activities, following a stage approach: visits to universities and research institutes in 1998; granting research contracts in 1999; creating a first research centre at Moscow State University in 2001; and, in subsequent years, creating a technology hub at Gubkin O&G University and an engineering centre at Akadengorodok. This very active outsourcing strategy has already given birth to 40 collaborative projects that engage 280 scientists in areas of Russian strength, such as mathematics, numerical modelling techniques/simulation, geoscience, physics, reservoir engineering, experimentation of alternative techniques in the oilfield. In addition, Schlumberger contributes to the education of a new generation of scientists and engineers through various agreements (scholarships, PhD and post-doctoral grants) with top universities.

Box 2.4. **Restructuring research-intensive large state-owned firms: The case of Svetlana**

Svetlana, which was the leading producer of semi-conductors in the Soviet era, exemplifies the problem. Its Russian customers from the previous era now appear to be buying the bulk of their electronic components from abroad. It has an impressive portfolio of technological capabilities but ones which only lent themselves to exploitation in niche markets, by spinning out medium-sized firms, or via small spin-off companies. Many other large Russian science-based and engineering-based companies are probably in a similar situation as their customers replace Russian made goods with foreign ones. Companies whose customers are mainly in the government sector would appear to be doing better.

The number of small innovative enterprises is not large, considering the size of the Russian economy, and that of small R&D-performing SMEs is of course even much smaller. The framework conditions – tax, capital and financial markets, administrative barriers – inhibit the emergence of a vibrant SME sector. However a certain evolution in factors that small enterprises identify as hampering their innovative activity is noticeable (Table 2.4) and should inspire new policy initiatives.

Table 2.4. **Factors hampering SMEs' innovative activity**

Surveys of 1999 and 2000	Survey of 2003
Lack of financial resources (70% of surveyed)	Underdeveloped infrastructure in the area of technology commercialisation (46%)
Economic instability in the country (25%)	Incomplete and misleading legislation (22%)
Lack of modern equipment (20%)	Lack of financial resources (16%)

Source: Foundation for Assistance to Small Innovative Enterprises.

The consequences of the excessive fragmentation of a large part of the innovation system (public research organisations) and of the atrophy of some of its other components (university-based research and business R&D) are aggravated by the lack of linkages among the actors:

- Multiple steering and non-coordinated funding mechanisms, together with a wide geographical spread (Tables A1.2 and A1.3 in Annex 1), do not facilitate synergies among the large number of public research organisations themselves.
- Public research and higher education institutions are quite separate worlds. One reason is the underdevelopment of university-based research, as pointed out above. But there are also barriers which limit co-operation on "training for research" and "training by research" issues.[7]
- Inter-firm diffusion of knowledge and innovation through networking or markets for technologies is very insufficient, compared to the situation in OECD countries (Box A1.1 in Annex 1). In the Soviet era, the central planning system inhibited networking between firms, particularly between customers and suppliers, and made it unnecessary for industrial firms to develop modern marketing capabilities. This now adds to their difficulty in competing in international markets and makes them weak in a business capability crucial for successful innovation. Whereas the diffusion process seems to have improved rapidly for soft innovation (modern production processes, business cultures and models, design,

7. The government is aware of the need to improve the situation. In 1996, a programme entitled "The State Support of the Integration of Higher Education and Fundamental Science for 1997-2000" was initiated by the Ministry of Education and the Russian Academy of Sciences. In 2000, the programme, renamed "Integration of Science and Higher Education in Russia", was prolonged to the year 2006 and extended to cover university-industry relations.

marketing and branding introduced first by foreign companies and subsequently adopted and disseminated by Russian ones) in some sectors,[8] many bottlenecks obstruct the diffusion the domestically grown technological innovation.

- Weak industry-science relationships (ISRs) are preventing Russia from making the best use of its considerable human and knowledge capital. Islands of science-based innovation are not only small but rather isolated from each other and from potential end users which could transform their results into wealth by expanding existing markets or creating new ones. ISRs appear to be sporadic, reflecting the lack of absorptive capacity in industry but also the inexperience of the research sector regarding the transfer of technology and knowledge and the lack of appropriate institutional frameworks.

Deficient incentives and lack of intermediation

Some of the basic incentives that in OECD countries ensure a minimal degree of coherence between the individual actions of the main players in the innovation system are not properly in place in Russia:

- *Inefficient funding mechanisms*. Such mechanisms play a key role in ensuring the quality of research, in securing critical mass throughout the research system, in avoiding unwarranted drifts in the research agenda of individual research institutes (*e.g.* too near-market development work to the detriment of more ambitious R&D), and in promoting co-operation among them. In Russia, the funding of public research organisations is not provided as part of a systematic policy. The state funding of R&D results from a combination of budgetary channels and programmes whose objectives and priorities are set independently. As a result, the individual research institutes operate opportunistically in seeking funding via contracts from the private industry, from state enterprises and the rest of the public sector or from innovation support programmes. Many organisations (and to some extent, individuals

---

8. Foreign investment is primarily oriented towards raw material-extracting and processing industry (*e.g.* oil, forestry). However, it also plays a key role in some other sectors, *e.g.* ICTs and food and beverages, in introducing best production and marketing practices. But there are now private Russian firms which are capable of spreading them across sectors. The OECD mission interviewed one of these firms, Russian Standard. Not only was it successful in introducing process and organisational innovation in the beverage industry, but it is now contributing to innovation in the banking and insurance sectors.

within organisations) have tended to develop their own "local innovation systems" which cannot not add up to a coherent macro system.

- *Uncertainties regarding the ownership of tangible and intangible assets* (*e.g.* IPRs). Such uncertainties complicate collaboration of research institutes with private firms, inhibit technology transfer, impair the development of spin-off companies into independent and growing businesses, create conflicts of interest for institutes themselves, and may even give rise to conflicting goals between individual researchers and their organisations. Intellectual property rights allocation is currently one of the most discussed problems in Russian science and technology policy. The discussions centre around regulations of intellectual property (IP) created with budget expenditures. There is still no transparent legal basis for allocation of such IP. At present, there are important contradictions between the Patent Law and legislation on public procurement. A draft new law that would resolve these contradictions by transferring IP ownership to research institutions has been approved by the Council of Ministers but has not yet been officially enacted. The use and disposal of tangible assets theoretically owned by the state is poorly regulated in practice, since it is difficult to exercise control over the more than 10 000 currently existing state-owned enterprises (the so-called "unitary enterprises").

Box 2.5. **A meeting place for innovators: The Innovation-Technology Centre (ITC) of the University of St. Petersburg**

The innovation-technology centre (ITC) of the St. Petersburg University of Information Technologies, Mechanics and Optics has been established with the support of regional authorities, federal programmes and industry. It is hosted on the premises of the Vavilov Research Institute for Optics, whose director is also General Manager of the ITC. In addition to being an incubator of new science-based firms, it provides a meeting place where individual firms, venture capitalists, business associations (*e.g.* Fort Ross consortium in the area of software), public research and teaching institutions (both scientific and engineering departments and business schools), as well as regional policy makers can co-ordinate their actions to their mutual benefit.

Box 2.6. **Technology parks and innovation technology centres (ITCs): A mixed experience**

Technological parks were among the first elements of new the innovative infrastructure in Russia. They emerged in the late 1980s. Currently 78 technology parks are active, mostly as extensions of universities. However, only 30 of them passed the accreditation in 2000.

In general, they unite small innovating enterprises and provide them first with office space at a rate below the market price for a limited time and, secondly, arrange consulting services for them such as auditing, business plan drafting, access to telecommunications, and assistance in fundraising. They were supported mainly by the former Ministry of Education (the larger share) and the Foundation for Assistance to Small Innovative Enterprises (FASIE) with, sometimes, a contribution by local authorities, but very rarely by industrial enterprises.

The concept of technology parks was modelled on Western experience but its adaptation to Russian conditions was not very successful because it was done at a time when market mechanisms were not yet in place. Therefore, in 1997, a new attempt was undertaken by the Russian government, aimed to create more effectively functioning infrastructure. These were ITCs.

ITCs represent conglomerates of small innovating enterprises which are located in compact territory. Most of participating firms are involved in the manufacturing stage and only a small number are pure R&D organisations. Some ITCs were created on the basis of technology parks and all of them provide similar services.

Today there are 52 such Centres in different regions of Russia which host more than 1000 SMEs. Some ITCs were established based exclusively on federal support while others benefited from combined federal and regional sponsoring. This is a very modest infrastructure if one takes into account the size of the Russian economy.

The evaluation of ITCs conducted in 2001 revealed that for small enterprises the most attractive features in ITCs are: privileged renting conditions, possibility to take part in investment programmes, and geographical location. As much less important were ranked such resources as training programmes, consulting services, and exchange of experience with the other on-site small enterprises. This may be partly explained by the fact that currently, professional consulting and training services are affordable outside ITCs, sometimes at lower prices.

- Market-based technological services as well as non-profit intermediary institutions which connect suppliers and users of knowledge are insufficiently developed. These are essential components of a well-functioning infrastructure for knowledge transmission and for sharing among actors of innovation processes. In Russia, inadequate legislation of IPRs limits the scope of market transactions of codified knowledge (patents and licensing).[9] Also, correcting misinformation regarding who has and who needs specific technological capabilities or know-how makes the living of a myriad of private consultants working for single clients, but incorrect information is not sufficiently corrected through co-operative action by business associations, multi-purpose innovation centres created at the initiative of local actors (Box 2.5), specialised government-sponsored non-profit organisations, or by public funding agencies as a by-product of their main activity. Support programme experience is this field is rather mixed (Box 2.6).

Adverse framework conditions

An innovation system evolves and is the product of national history, culture, norms, laws and values, resource endowments, patterns of production, etc. The forces which drive the evolution of the system are complex. However, public sector institutions such as universities, public sector research organisations, schools, regulatory bodies, public purchasers, monetary authorities, laws, the fiscal system, etc., all play key roles, whether positive or negative, in determining innovation. The government has a vital role in ensuring that policies towards these institutions are innovation-friendly and that they reinforce rather than counteract each other.

Innovators in Russia do not enjoy fully supportive business, financial, regulatory and policy environments. They are handicapped by the competition for financial and human resources, and the expansion of the markets for their products and services is constrained by several factors. They suffer from the malfunctioning of three basic mechanisms of an efficient dynamic allocation of resources: corporate governance that ensures forward-looking re-investment of earnings; a financial system that is capable of managing the risks of innovation-related investment; and an active government policy to use part of the economic rents from exports of raw materials to finance

9. Six technology transfer centres (TTCs) have recently been created in six regions as part of a pilot programme to promote commercialisation of R&D results using public funds.

investments in the knowledge infrastructure through an ambitious technology and innovation policy. The most important hindrances are:

- Excessive returns in low risk/non-innovative activities (due to, for example, lack of competition or inadequate regulation), together with legal uncertainties (*e.g.* regarding IPRs) that increase transaction costs within the innovation system, reduce the incentives of cash-rich firms and financial institutions to invest in innovation.
- The weakness of the banking system, and the small size of financial markets, including an embryonic venture capital (Box 2.7).
- Lack of consistency of different policies regarding their impact on innovation (*e.g.* trade policy,[10] labour legislation, procurement policy, tax policy, *etc.*).
- A grey area (which is still large) between the private and public sectors where actors have a legal status and governance structures which are not the most appropriate to make them either efficient market players or efficient components of the knowledge infrastructure.
- Lack of a clear government commitment and strategy to improve such framework conditions, as part of an explicit and comprehensive technology and innovation policy. There is a striking contrast between official statements regarding the need to initiate a new growth trajectory in order to double the GDP and rather patchy innovation policy initiatives.

10. The structure of tariffs may impair the marketing of new products by young highly innovative firms. For example, crystals grown through leading-edge science-based processes (an important field of innovation where Russia could build a comparative advantage) are considered as semi-precious stones and their export is taxed.

Box 2.7. **Venture capital in Russia**

Venture capital markets in Russia started to surface in the early 1990s, when large institutional investors from abroad appeared in the country. Between 1994 and 1998, about USD 3 billion was invested, of which only 3% came from Russian sources.

After the financial crisis of August 1998 some foreign investors left Russia, which led to shrinking funding: between 1999 and 2004 investment went just slightly over USD 1 billion. At the same time, venture funds operating in different Russian regions merged and consolidated their activities. Only the strongest among managing companies stayed on the market, such as Quadriga Capital from Germany, Eagle from Holland and the Scandinavian company Norum.

The downturn in foreign capital activities was partially compensated by growing interest among Russian investors – between 1999 and 2004, Russian sources accounted for 26% of all invested funds. The most active players among Russian investors are industrial companies and banks. The government's role in the past years has been limited to establishing the Venture Innovation Foundation – "a funds of funds" – through which the state intends to participate in establishing new commercial venture funds that invest in innovation in different fields. The share of the Venture Innovation Foundation in each newly created commercial fund shall not exceed 10%. Only one commercial venture fund, operating in the airspace and defence sector,s has been established so far.

Up to 1998 the largest investments were made in communications, packaging, breweries and the food industry. Investment in high-tech industries was very marginal during this period. The situation has changed since then, and between 1999 and 2004 investment in high-tech reached about 20% of all invested funds. The breakdown of venture investment per business phase indicates that investment in expansion of already established companies clearly prevails today. The high risk component of investment in Russia remains extremely small.

An important player on the Russian venture capital market is the Russian Private Equity and Venture Capital Association. The Association was established in 1997 at the initiative of regional (Russian) venture foundations of the European Bank for Reconstruction and Development. Members are investment companies and other organisations operating on the Russian venture capital market: Delta Capital, Agribusiness, Quadriga Capital, Norum, etc.

According to the Russian Private Equity and Venture Capital Association, the northwest is one of the most lucrative regions in Russia as far as venture investment is concerned. But overall the average yield throughout the entire Russian venture market is only 11% per annum today.

Box 2.7. **Venture capital in Russia** *(continued)*

Figure 2.5. **Breakdown of investments by sector (USD millions) and stage (%), 1994-2004**

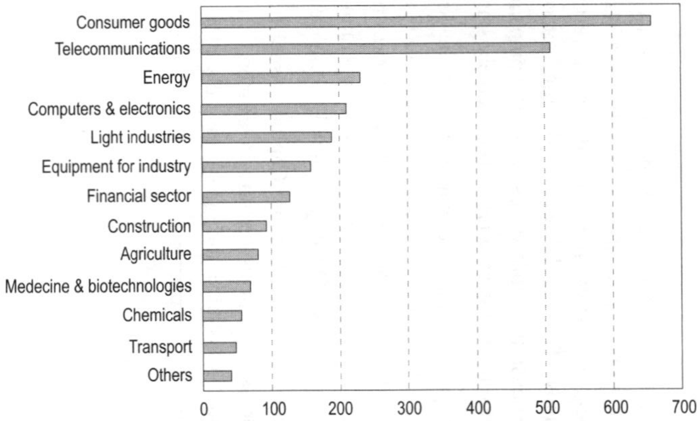

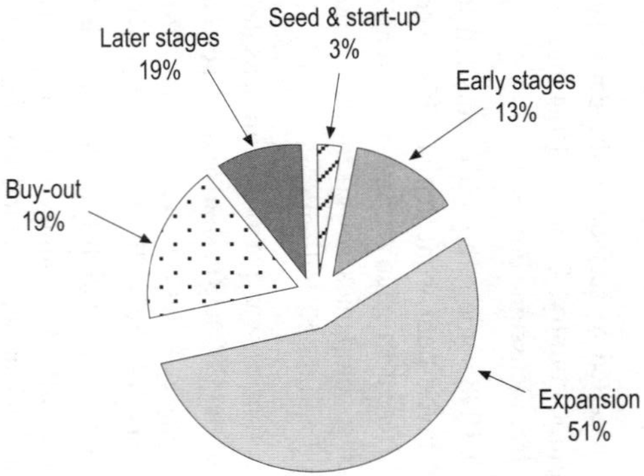

Source: Russian Private Equity and Venture Capital Association, 2004.

Opportunities

The fact that under such conditions R&D-intensive activities are flourishing in some sectors, notably information technologies and telecommunications (ICTs), and that technological upgrading and organisational innovation has been very successful in others, *e.g.* some segments of the food and chemical industries, is an indication that Russia has the necessary capabilities, *e.g.* in terms of entrepreneurial spirit and highly skilled labour, to position itself favourably in global innovation networks once certain key requirements are met.

So far, real successes have occurred in relatively new industries that have emerged in the last decade and were therefore less dependent on the legacy of the Soviet period, or in sectors where a booming domestic demand soon attracted foreign direct investors or facilitated foreign technology transfers. In addition, sizeable high-tech clusters have been nurtured in large cities, especially Moscow and St. Petersburg, where there is a sufficient critical mass of universities and research institutions in addition to fairly good infrastructures, competition and opportunities to co-operate, industrial clients, and an attractive residential environment.

Such conditions cannot be replicated elsewhere but there are many locations and sectors where the basic ingredients for a dynamic clustering process await only some complementary resources and catalytic measures (see Box 2.8). For example, in the so-called science towns, an injection of business management skills would allow to extract more economic value from existing assets: strong research institutes, well-equipped laboratories and test factories, scientific traditions, and international connections. Scientific capabilities developed during the Soviet Union to serve the defence industrial complex, space industry and aviation could provide the basis for new innovative clusters if entrepreneurial ventures can develop relevant product innovations and efficient manufacturing for civil markets. The demand of the raw material-based industries might give birth to more knowledge-intensive services. The forthcoming pick-up in investment will provide opportunities for innovators in machinery and equipment.

Box 2.8. **Emerging and latent innovative clusters in Russia**

Main geographical locations

a. *Moscow and St. Petersburg* are the most important locations in the clustering process. In these cities many potential clusters are developing, which cover nearly all the industries and technologies in which Russia is somehow competitive. They include optics, nanotechnologies, nuclear technologies, energy technologies, shipbuilding, laser technologies, biotechnologies (primarily in pharmaceutics), information technologies (math modelling, speech recognition and production systems, as well as those for text and image, information security, etc.), development of new materials (in particular, special alloys and polymers), space technologies, technologies of personal safety, a whole range of specialized technologies in the field of prospecting and extraction of mineral wealth, and of course military technologies.

b. Many other *large cities* represent the "home base" for one or several industry technologies: for example Ekaterinburg (metallurgy), Nizhni Novgorod (car industry, shipbuilding), Perm (petrochemistry), Samara (space technologies and car industry), Voronezh (aviation technologies), etc.

c. Several *science towns* (small towns with high concentration of R&D activity in certain fields) are very important generators of knowledge and could become a center of science-intensive clusters.

- Nuclear technologies: Dubna, Obninsk, Protvino, Sosnovy Bor, *etc.*
- Biotechnologies: Krasnoobsk, Obolensk, Puschino, Koltsovo.
- Space and rocket technologies: Korolev, Himki, Reutov, Ubileini, Krasnoznamensk, Zvezdni, *etc.*
- Aviation: Zhukovski, Lytkarino.
- Radio-electronics and micro-electronics: Frjazino, Zelenograd.
- Defence industries: Krasnoarmeisk, Klimovsk, and many others.
- Fundamental science: Chernogolovka, Troitsk, Novosibirsk RAS Centre.

d. *10 closed towns* specialized in military-related research and production should be mentioned separately. They in fact represent "strong and very cohesive clusters" but work under public procurement only.

- Sarov
- Snezhinsk
- Zarechni
- Zheleznogorsk
- Novouralsk
- Ozerk
- Lesnoy
- Zelenogorsk
- Trehgorni
- Seversk

Box 2.8. **Emerging and latent innovative clusters in Russia** *(continued)*

Sectoral clusters in specific locations

- St. Petersburg optics and optoelectronics cluster (ITMO, LOMO, State Optical Institute).
- St. Petersburg power engineering cluster ("Power Machines", State Technical University, Polzunov CKTI, etc.).
- St. Petersburg shipbuilding cluster (Admiralteiskie Shipyards, Baltijski Zavod, Severnays Shipyard, Krylov CNII, CKB Rubin, NPO Almaz, *etc.*)
- St. Petersburg IT cluster (technical universities and many specialized small and medium-sized companies).
- Moscow space technology cluster (Moscow Aviation Institute, Moscow State Technical University named after Bauman, Institute for Space Research, Tracking Headquarters, Energia corporation, Design Bureau Himmash).
- Moscow radio-electronics cluster (Moscow Institute for Electronics, Radio Technology and Automatics, Moscow State Technical University named after Bauman, Technical University for Communications and Informatics).
- Ekaterinburg metallurgy and metal working cluster (Uralmash, Urals Polytechnical Institute).
- Tatarstan oil processing cluster (KazanOrgsintez, Nizhnekamskneftehim, Nizhnekamskshina, Tatneft, Kazan State University).
- Zelenograd electronics cluster (Zelenograd Science and Technology Park, Moscow State Institute for Electronics, AFK Systema).
- Dubna nuclear studies and instrumentation cluster (Institute for Nuclear Studies, Dubna Machine Building Plant, Instrumentation Plant Tensor, NII Atoll).
- Koltsovo biotech cluster (Centre for Biotechnologies Vector, Novosibirsk State University).

New science-based firms are important players in most high-tech industries. There are around 30 000 small companies involved in some form of R&D in Russia. This may seem a high figure, but to put it in perspective, it represents no more than about eight times the number of public research organisations. There is thus a need and large room for the creation of new ones. Spin-offs from public research organisations should play a key role here. They are efficient channels to commercialise results from public research, contribute to change the mindsets in research organisations, attract people with business skills in the vicinity of knowledge institutions, and can help trigger a clustering process around them. However, alone they cannot transform a science city or a dying state-owned enterprise into a vibrant innovative cluster (Box 2.9) unless some of them can grow rapidly to become medium-sized firms and/or partner with large firms that have complementary assets in manufacturing and marketing. There are two hurdles to be overcome. One is at the creation and incubation stage. The only sizeable, but still small, source of seed and start-up financing is the Foundation for Assistance to Small Innovative Enterprises. Another hurdle is at the initiation of the growth phase. The disappointing experience of venture capital funds demonstrates that such a hurdle is very high in Russia (Box 2.7). The Russian venture market for high-tech investment is in its infancy. The infrastructure of venture financing is not sufficiently developed: it lacks efficient managing companies, specialists in technological rating and legal frameworks to guide transactions, etc. The small scale of Russian innovation projects has so far not attracted large Russian investors. The government has taken only initial steps towards stimulating venture funding of technology, but has not yet formulated any clear development priorities.

Box 2.9. **Spin-offs from public research: Lessons from case studies**

The OECD mission visited two sites where the two main Russian public research spin-off models were implemented: spin-offs from Institutes of the Academy of Sciences (in the science town of Chernogolovka), and spin-offs from a former large high-tech state-owned enterprise (Svetlana in St. Petersburg, which used to be the largest electronics company in the country). They are both active in the creation of new technology-based firms (NTBFs) and are acting as 'incubators' for such companies. They can also transform themselves into an innovation centre (*e.g.* the Innovation-Technology Centre of the St. Petersburg Regional Foundation for Scientific and Technological Development, hosted on the Svetlana premises) that can attract new firms based on outside knowledge. Svetlana can indeed be regarded as a holding company of new businesses. One key enabling factor is the possession of unused land, buildings and equipment as a result of the substantial decline in funding and, in the case of Svetlana, the loss of customers following the end of the Soviet era.

Spin-off business have a number of advantages:

- Premises provided at cheap rents.
- Free use of institute facilities.
- Dual employment of business founder.
- Access to know-how and research results.
- Public sector R&D contracts (including engineering and software development).

Typical outputs of spin-off businesses include:

- Novel materials, many of which are for research use.
- Specialised engineering components and products.
- Small-scale production of devices.
- Software development and customisation of software licensed from abroad for Russian customers.

In other words, this is a collection of small-scale businesses selling in niches or highly specialised markets. In some cases licenses are granted to foreign companies. Production is on laboratory or small workshop scale. Some of the businesses appear to have good technological contacts with overseas companies.

Box 2.9. **Spin-offs from public research: Lessons from case studies** ***(continued)***

Because of the advantages listed above, these businesses remain attached to the institutes which spawn them. Institute directors in turn see them as a means of retaining staff on the premises, increasing their remuneration and providing an excuse to retain land, premises and facilities which would otherwise be wholly or partly redundant. Institute directors are often either shareholders or non-executive directors.

An important reason why commercial exploitation of research results has taken this form is that both the physical and intellectual property possessed by institutes (and state enterprises such as Svetlana) belong to the Russian Federation and cannot be transferred to private enterprises.

These two models seem to have some limitations. First, institutes may not have adequate incentives to transfer knowledge and technology to a wider group of new technology-based firms, including those originating elsewhere. Acting as a holding company/incubator for daughter companies creates conflicts of interest which may preclude this role. Means should be found to separate the institutes' scientific role from their incubator role without destroying the valuable links from the former to the latter. Secondly, in the case of Svetlana, the very cheap rents for expensive land and office spaces may create unfair competition with other sound initiatives, may not represent the best economic use of these public assets and, furthermore, may delay the necessary decisions regarding the privatisation or dismantling of the remaining research and manufacturing activities of the state-owned company.

Chapter 3

RUSSIAN INNOVATION POLICY: ACHIEVEMENTS AND SHORTCOMINGS

An unclear overall strategy

The experience of OECD countries demonstrates that: *1)* government has a vital role in promoting an innovation-led growth since innovation processes are affected by endemic market and systemic failures which need to be corrected; and *2)* government promotion of innovation requires the contribution of different policies according to a coherent overall strategy. The Russian government has the additional task of completing or consolidating the institutional frameworks, including legal, regulatory and incentive frameworks, which underpin the innovation systems of mature market economies.

The Russian government has ambitious economic development goals and is well aware of the need to enhance innovation capabilities in order to fulfil them. However, it does not yet have a clear overall strategy or all the necessary policy tools in order to boost innovation.[1] It has so far employed a variety of different instruments in pursuing its technology and innovation policy. Such experimentation is entirely appropriate, particularly as the design and implementation of innovation policy is, in comparison with most OECD countries, at an early stage. However, there needs to be a framework for monitoring and learning from policy actions. Russia should develop its own systematic approach to the *ex ante* appraisal, with concurrent moni-

1. The Russian government has repeatedly stated in recent years that it pursues the development of a national innovation system. The document of the most general nature that outlines a strategy in this respect is entitles "The Foundations of Policy of the Russian Federation in the Field of Development of Science and Technology for the Period up to 2010 and More Remote Prospects". This document, which was endorsed by President Putin in March 2002, sets out guidelines for accelerating the transition from raw material-based development to an innovation-based model of growth. It is more in the nature of a declaration, without the necessary focus on the most urgent and manageable problems, and leaves unanswered the crucial question of the elaboration of appropriate tools to achieve the proclaimed goals.

toring and *ex post* evaluation of all innovation policy instruments and schemes in order to continuously check and improve the basic framework conditions for innovation when necessary.

Boosting innovation is a continuous and unending process, which in most countries often only requires fine tuning and improved co-ordination of policies in areas such as such as science and technology, macro-economic management, education, competition, corporate governance, labour markets, energy, banking and financial markets, IPRs, etc. In Russia, the challenge is greater since its transformation into a full-fledged market economy is still underway. It would be beyond the scope of this report to discuss in detail all aspects of this transformation that are important from an innovation perspective. However, certain areas should receive priority attention.

The mechanisms for inter-ministerial co-ordination on innovation issues are presently inadequate. The newly established Council on Competitiveness and Entrepreneurship may help improve such co-ordination, provided that it is entrusted with a truly substantive agenda. This includes a role in defining a clearer national technology and innovation policy strategy, streamlining and co-ordinating government support to R&D that involves several ministries, and ensuring that broad reforms in other fields are consistent with the national innovation strategy.[2] More effective inter-ministerial co-ordination would be necessary, *inter alia*, in order to:

- Remove specific regulatory impediments to innovation. For example, one example that requires serious consideration is the regulation of domestic energy prices which still artificially increases comparative advantages enjoyed by energy-intensive export sectors to the detriment of knowledge-based activities, and reduces incentives for energy-saving innovations. Another example involves the possible inconsistencies between technological and environment policies. Some state-supported R&D may only have a slight chance to be commercialised due to the

2. These include competition policies to increase innovation-driving rivalry but also facilitate collaborative research; education and training policies to develop the necessary human capital; regulatory reform policies to lessen administrative burdens and institutional rigidities; financial and fiscal policies to ease the flow of capital to small innovative firms; labour market policies to increase the mobility of personnel and strengthen tacit knowledge flows; communications policies to maximise the dissemination of information and enable the growth of electronic networks; foreign investment and trade policies to strengthen technology diffusion; and regional policies to improve complementarity between different levels of government initiatives.

state of legislation (and enforcement) in the area of environmental protection.[3]

- Define a pro-innovation procurement policy. Despite some recent improvements in the system of state R&D contracts, there are neither clear, agreed principles nor an articulated strategy concerning the role of the public sector as lead user of innovation through procurement policy.
- Rectify the policy implementation gap in areas where the government knows perfectly what should be done and has the willingness to do it, but faces obstacles in the legislative or budgetary process or, later on, at the implementation stage. In particular, the draft new law on IPRs derived from publicly funded research, which transfers ownership to the research institutions, is a good initiative which follows international best practices but has not yet been officially enacted.

The specific contribution of science and technology policy is central in any innovation strategy. The main objectives, in broad terms, have no reason to be different in Russia than in OECD countries, namely: to support basic and long-term research while ensuring that it is responsive to the evolving needs of the economy and society; to correct market failures which lead business firms to under-invest in R&D and innovation; to provide the infrastructures needed for the diffusion of knowledge and technologies throughout the economy; to promote co-operation among all actors to fill gaps in research capabilities; and to foster innovation in areas of strategic interest. But the prioritisation and nature of specific actions to achieve these objectives need to reflect specific Russian conditions.

A first observation is the government does not seem to have full knowledge of such conditions, which would require more indicators and information (*e.g.* on privately financed and performed R&D, spin-offs, licensing, human resource mobility) in order to adhere to a more evidence-based approach to policy making. Second, and more importantly, science and technology policy in Russia is insufficiently oriented towards innovation, because political energy, budgets, administrative means and lobbying efforts by vested interests are spent primarily in two other directions: the administration and funding of the science system, and the procurement of R&D and technologies by the administration and a very large state-owned industrial sector. Probably less than 10% of the total federal budget for R&D is available for supporting science-based technological innovation (see Figure 3.1 and Table 3.1). Whereas innovation is now recognised as a vital

3. This has led to criticism about the relevance of some Megaprojects supported by the Ministry of Education and Science.

issue from a policy perspective, it remains an "orphan subject" from an institutional point of view. This problem exists to some degree in all OECD countries, but it is more acute in Russia, for three reasons: the legacy of the science-technology-industry model of the Soviet period, the dual steering of the science system (Ministries/Russian Academies), and the limited size and influence of the R&D-intensive private sector.

Fostering industry-science relationships: a priority task

In all OECD countries ISRs are becoming increasingly important (see Box 3.1). Science contributes more regularly and more directly to industrial innovation today than in the past. The changing nature of scientific research makes earlier distinctions between basic and applied research less clear and less policy-relevant. An effective interface between innovation and science systems is therefore more necessary than ever to reap broad economic and social benefits from public and private investments in research and to ensure the vitality and quality of the science system itself.

In Russia, there are additional reasons to attach the highest priority to the improvement of ISRs since this would trigger other desirable changes in the research and productive systems, such as increased propensity of firms to invest in R&D, competitive selection of high quality fundamental research with economic relevance, concentration of resources in selected fields of strategic importance for the economy and society, and consolidation of the public R&D system through improved collaboration between institutes with complementary capabilities.

In fact, promoting ISRs is a focused but also integrative policy agenda which can help federate almost all other objectives of science, technology and innovation policy (Figure 3.2). There are many channels of ISRs (informal contacts, spin-offs, mobility of researchers, collaborative research, licensing, contact research) and several ways for government to strengthen each of them. Russia has not yet devised its own overall coherent strategy to increase the intensity and quality of ISRs by combining different policy tools: regulatory reform, institutional building, public-private partnership programmes and financial incentives.

Figure 3.1. **Sources of R&D financing in 2002**

Percentage of total (USD 5 750 million)

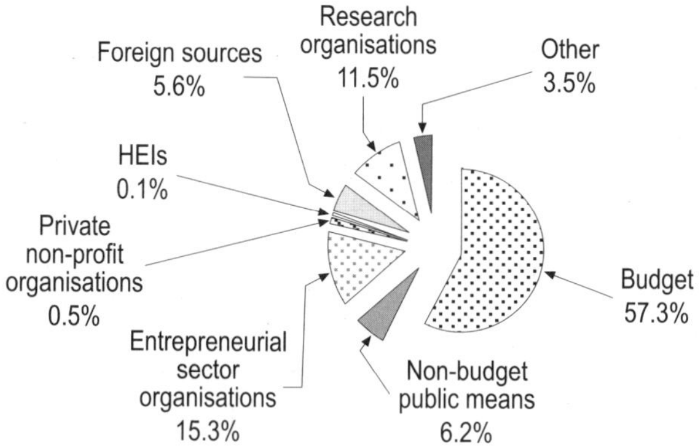

Table 3.1. **Federal budget for "Basic Research and Scientific and Technological Progress"**

2002, USD millions

Total	956
Ministries and agencies	294
Academies of Sciences	411
Goal-oriented budgetary foundations	78
Russian Foundation for Basic Research	*55*
Russian Foundation for Humanities	*9*
Foundation for Assistance to Small Innovative Enterprises	*14*
Priority directions for science and technology development	173
Financing R&D of federal goal-oriented programmes	*84*
International projects and programmes, support to international scientific and technological cooperation	*18*
Creation of communication networks and databases for basic science and education	*6*
Others	*65*

Source: Goskomstat.

Box 3.1. **Intensity and quality of industry-science relationships (ISRs): Key determinants of the efficiency of national innovation systems**

The science base of a country includes universities, research institutes and departments, other public sector research organisations (PROs) and private firms and independent foundations which undertake contract research or provide high-level scientific and technological advice and consultancy. More broadly, it may be useful to also include teaching departments particularly where these are closely integrated with research functions. The term 'science' mainly refers to natural and engineering sciences, but social science has a role to play as well.

Industry should be taken to include not just manufacturing, energy and construction but also services, agriculture, trading organisations and utilities in the public sector as well as government departments, *i.e.* business both public and private. Most of these organisations are private commercial firms but the proportion will vary according to where the division between the public and private sectors is drawn in the country concerned.

The science base generates a number of important benefits for business:

- Highly qualified people including trained researchers.
- Research results which form the basis for research-based (as opposed to engineering-based) technologies used in business.
- Analytical methods and approaches which can be used to solve a wide range of technological and business problems.
- Test and measurement methods and prototype equipment.
- A stock of scientific and technological expertise which business can access.
- A source of new spin-off companies.

These benefits can flow through a variety of means:

- Informal networks frequently based on personal contacts.
- Formal networks provided by professional associations, committees whose memberships include both scientists and businessmen, etc.
- Mobility of qualified scientists and engineers.
- Publication in journals, research reports, conferences, seminars, *etc.*
- Research and consultancy contracts placed by business with the science base.
- Joint research and other forms of partnership.

These forms of contact vary from informal relationships with relatively little commitment on either side to formal partnerships supported by legally enforced contracts or agreements. Evaluations suggest that trust based on previous experience of working with a partner or partners is important in ensuring the effectiveness of ISRs, and that effective partnerships between universities/PROs and business firms usually develop organically. Trust plus shared objectives and interests provide a better basis for ISRs than formal legal agreements. The development of regular contacts and ongoing relationships is therefore important.

Box 3.1. **Intensity and quality of industry-science relationships (ISRs): Key determinants of the efficiency of national innovation systems**
(continued)

More broadly, the effectiveness of ISRs depends on:

- The quality, extent and relevance of the knowledge possessed by the science base, and the incentives for individual scientists, research centres and universities to work with business and the legal and administrative framework in which researchers operate.
- The extent, variety and strength of the various ways in which science and business interact (see discussion earlier in this chapter).
- The ability and willingness of business organisations to exploit the outputs of the science base.

ISRs are becoming increasingly important for the following reasons:

- Science-based technologies such as electronics, pharmacology, biotechnology and nanotechnology are becoming increasingly important and have moved to the forefront of innovation.
- The rise of computer-aided design and computer-aided manufacture (CADCAM) has resulted in a move away from craft-based technology to technology based on more formal bodies of knowledge in many traditional engineering sectors.
- The horizontal spread of science-based technologies such as new materials, new coatings and adhesives, advanced analytical and measurement methods, catalysts based on nanoscience including to many traditional industrial sectors.

Individual products and processes are incorporating an increasing range of technologies, and even the largest firms are having to source technological knowledge and research from outside.

The currently very low intensity of ISRs, their geographical rather than sectoral or techno-scientific polarisation, and the disproportionate importance of informal channels suggest that, in addition to the improvement of framework conditions,[4] resolute measures need to be taken simultaneously on two fronts in order to:

- Make the actors more attractive and motivated partners (laying the ground).
- Promote their collaboration (public-private partnerships).

4. An IPR regime which facilitates knowledge transfers, spin-offs and joint R&D; regulatory reforms to improve the mobility of human resources; improved priority setting in S&T policy, etc.

Figure 3.2. **The Russian model of ISRs**

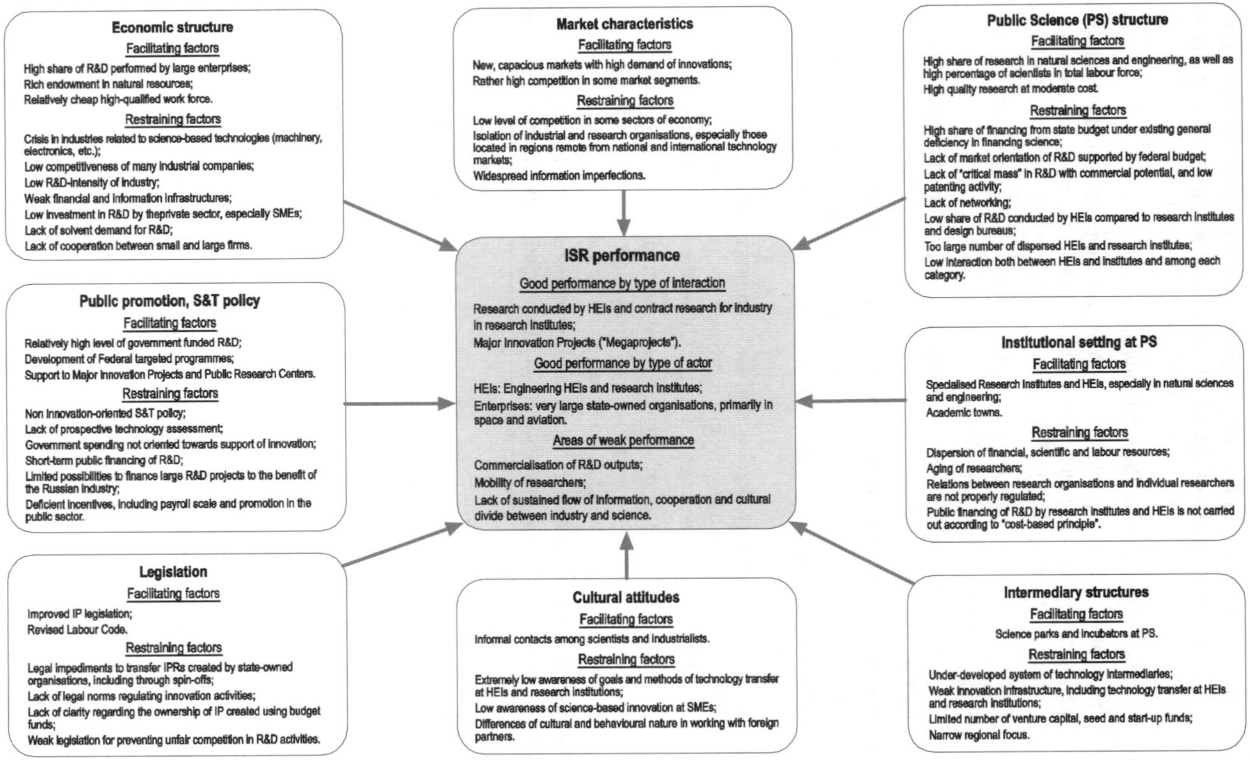

Laying the ground

Many public research organisations are ill-prepared to enter into fruitful relationships with the private sector. The situation has improved in recent years and the government has taken measures that could accelerate the required changes, but some are still ill-defined or immature while others lack the scale to have a sizeable impact.

The restructuring of public research organisations (PROs) is still lagging,[5] but new initiatives are in the pipeline. An inventory and assessment of PROs belonging to the Russian Federation has been recently completed, including strategic directions for the improvement of steering mechanisms, privatisation of some PROs and liquidation of others. This new restructuring plan, announced by the Ministry of Education and Science in September 2004, is far more ambitious than any earlier plan and could radically change the face of the Russian R&D system: out of more than 2 000 organisations engaged in research and development, only 400-700 should still be government property by 2008. From these, 100-200 will be leading R&D institutes, and 300-500 will provide science services. A question which arises is whether such downsizing will be matched and facilitated by congruent developments in the private industrial sector (*e.g.* rapid growth of in-house R&D). Complementary measures to trigger such developments might be needed, in the form of tax incentives or grant-based schemes to stimulate business R&D and facilitate the transfer of human resources from the public to the private sector.

To be an attractive partner, public research must have capabilities that complement, and do not substitute industrial research. *Refocusing Russian PROs on fundamental long-term research and involving more real end users in their financing* is in this regard an absolute requirement. This will

5. There were several attempts to reform the organisational structure of the public research sector, but these were only partially successful, largely because several ministries, agencies and academies pursued unco-ordinated policies. In fact, the number of R&D institutes increased by 30% between 1992 and 2002; the only drastic streamlining occurred in the field of applied research and pure development (design bureaus, development organisations) (see Table 2.3). For example, in 2003 the RAS closed 45 institutes but an almost equal number were opened, and some institutes were disintegrated into several smaller legal entities. The former Ministry of Industry, Science and Technology conducted an inventory of R&D organisations in 2002 and developed a concept for reform but did put it into practice.

hopefully be facilitated by the current restructuring of PROs (as discussed above). However, this selection and consolidation process cannot be achieved suddenly and should be encouraged on a continuous basis for quite a long period through improved funding mechanisms.

Figure 3.3. **The financing sources of RAS institutes**

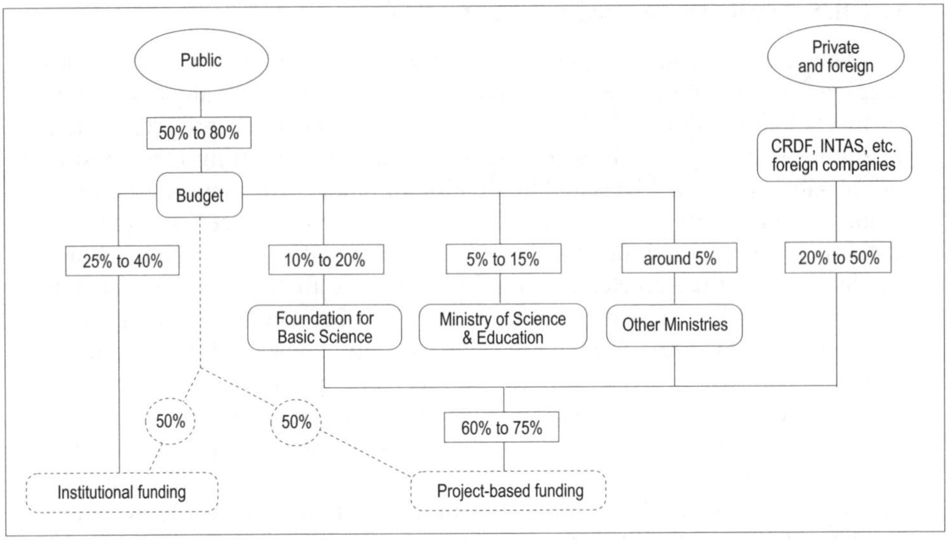

Source: Interview with academician Aldoshin.

Funding mechanisms should ensure that developmental activities are further reduced (abandoned, taken over by the productive sector, and only pursued in areas of strictly defined national interest), that applied research is only pursued when there are clear public or private end users ready to co-finance, and that basic and long-term research is supported subject to strict conditions regarding quality, critical mass and links with education. Overall, in a typical OECD country, this would entail greater use of project funding (typically contracts and grants awarded through competition), as opposed to institutional block grants.[6]

6. See *Governance of Science Systems: Towards Better Practices*, OECD, 2003.

For Russia, the implications are more complex, as are the current funding mechanisms themselves. It seems in fact that *both institutional and truly competitive funding are insufficiently developed* compared to other streams of project-based funding. The latter are multiple, including R&D contracts with public and private organisations, targeted programmes of different ministries, with not always transparent selection procedures and criteria, and international sources (Figure 3.3). Foundations, which implement the purest form of competitive allocation of funds, have a rather modest budget which, in addition, is spread on too many small projects (see Box 3.2). They can hardly have a strong structuring effect on the direction and quality of public research. The international sources of funding reached a peak in the late 1990s but since then have been declining both as a share of total R&D and in absolute terms, especially reflecting the sharp drop in funding from the United States (Table 3.2). This adds to the need to mobilise more national sources of funding while increasing the efficiency of spending through three priority actions: increasing the institutional funding of institutes with world-class capabilities; increasing the share of competitive grants within project-based funding; and increasing resources for the maintenance and renewal of research infrastructures.

Box 3.2. **Russian Federal Foundations to support research and technological development**

Grant-awarding foundations are the new main mechanisms of government support for R&D and innovation and were introduced in Russia during the early phase of the economic transformation. With their establishment, a new culture in the Russian research community started to develop. Like similar funds in Western countries, their main distinctive features compared to other funding instruments are: open competition for funds, bottom-up definition of research projects and accountability.

Russian Foundation for Basic Research (RFBR)

The RFBR was created in 1992. It supports basic research in all scientific fields. Its budget represents around 6% of government expenditures on civilian science. Today, the RFBR finances about 8 000 research projects in academic institutes, universities and industry. Over 2 000 researchers from different regions of Russia are involved in the peer review system of project selection. Each application is evaluated by up to 50 people.

RFBR is considered by researchers as a valuable source of funding for basic research and the purchase minor equipment. However, its relatively small budget considerably limits its structural impact on the research system.

Box 3.2. **Russian Federal Foundations to support research and technological development** *(continued)*

Russian Foundation for Humanities (RFH)

Initially, the RFH was a subdivision of the RFBR responsible for the support of social sciences and humanities. In 1994 it became an independent foundation. The RFH operates on the same principles as the RFBR, and its budget represents 1% of federal expenditure on civil science. The RFH faces the same problems as the RFBR: notably, a small budget, which is spread over too many projects.

Russian Foundation for Technological Development (RFTD)

Established in 1992, the RFTD operates under the auspices of the Ministry of Education and Science. A small levy on the production of industrial enterprises, together with reimbursements of its loans, makes up its budget (equivalent to 1.5-4% of total budgetary allocations for science).

In its selection process the Foundation uses the list of government priorities in high-tech areas. The Ministry also gives final approval to all projects.

The RFTD offers up to three-year interest-free credits through open competition to applied research projects which have an interdisciplinary and inter-industry application. The largest number of grantees come from the industry sector (about one-third) followed by the organisations of the Russian Academy of Sciences (10%) and higher education institutions.

At present, the RFTD is in a critical financial situation and has had to suspend new calls for proposals. The reason is the ongoing reform of all non-budgetary foundations, which led to the termination of payments to the RFTD.

Federal Fund for Assistance to Small Innovative Enterprises

This fund was created in 1994 as a federal organisation whose budget, according to the state law, equals 1.5% of federal allocations for civil science.

For a long period, the Fund focused its support on small innovating firms with a proven track record. In addition to providing project-based funding through rigorous competitive mechanisms (70% of its budget, 2 000 SMEs supported in 10 years), it has been very innovative in implementing several new approaches to support and stimulating innovative activity in small firms, *e.g.* management courses for small firms, including the fields of technology commercialisation and intellectual property rights protection, and the introduction in Russia of a scheme similar to the UK Teaching Company Scheme (TCS). It also initiated a pilot project in 1996 to support the creation of innovation technology centres (ITCs). In 2003, the Fund and the RFBR organised a joint call for proposals to support transfer of R&D results from PROs to small enterprises.

Late in 2003, the Fund initiated a new programme called START with the objective to facilitate the creation of new technology-based firms by researchers. The Fund provides research teams with “seed money”, and the goal of the first selection round was to support about 400 projects by the end of 2004.

Table 3.2. **Trends in foreign-financed Russian R&D**

Percentage of GERD

1995	1996	1997	1998	1999	2000	2001	2002
4.6	5.6	7.4	10.3	16.9	12.0	8.6	8.0

Source: Science in Russia at a Glance, Statistical Yearbook, 2000, 2002, 2003.

The *underdevelopment of university-based research* deprives Russia of a very effective springboard for ISRs. Research universities combine two powerful attractors of business interest: new knowledge – especially of a multidisciplinary nature – and qualified human resources. The experience of mature market economies also demonstrates that they form the best organisational framework for many types of R&D.[7] In the Soviet Union, teaching was by and large the sole function of universities. Even today, legally speaking, universities are not accredited as research institutions. The variety of research projects in which they may take part therefore remains limited. Until 2003, the higher education sector did not even receive budgetary support for basic research. The government has in the past taken small steps to bridge the gap between education and research (*e.g.* the Education Research Centres, see Box 3.3), and now appears determined to pursue more ambitious goals, but how it will act in practice is not yet entirely clear.

Box 3.3. **The Education Research Centres**

Education Research Centres (ERCs) have been created where joint work is undertaken by university professors, students and researchers from PROs. Today, 154 ERCs are functioning in almost all regions of Russia. In 2000, this programme, renamed "Integration of Science and Higher Education in Russia", was extended to cover university-industry relations. Its budget for 2002-2006 amounts to RUB 1 133 million (2001 prices), from which RUB 988 million comes from the state budget. This means that annual volume of budgetary support is no more than about USD 6.5 million. This is very small considering the number of ERCs and participating organisations (247 state universities, 320 RAS institutes, and 168 industrial R&D organisations). A larger budget and/or a concentration of support on fewer projects/recipients would seem desirable.

7. The OECD has provided some evidence that social return was on average greater for university-based research than for research in public laboratories.

An R&D-intensive and highly innovative private sector, which would play the leading role on the demand side of ISRs, is still the "sleeping beauty" of the Russian economy. Important policy emphasis has been placed on the promotion of small innovative firms, including new technology-based firms through project-based support, with the Federal Fund for Assistance to Small Innovative Enterprises (see Box 3.2) and support to incubators within PROs. These programmes are commendable, but can have only a relatively small and partial impact on economic structures and national innovation capabilities in the short to medium term. To have greater and quicker impact, they should be scaled up and complemented by initiatives that integrate SMEs in broader innovative networks comprising larger firms. The latter should be encouraged to increase their demand for science – rather than for technologies that they should develop themselves – from the public sector.

There needs to be a systematic policy towards building up the technological competence of state (and private) enterprises. Companies should consider to what extent the existing breadth and depth of their knowledge base can be maintained. They should identify those areas where, with the help of RAS institutes and/or universities, they can maintain their technology at the leading edge; other areas should be abandoned. Each state company could be asked to draw up a strategy for developing its technological competences including a full description of the external links which it proposes to exploit. This would include joint research projects with RAS institutes/Russian universities as well as a plausible business plan for exploitation (which could involve partnerships with foreign-based companies). Subject to independent appraisal such plans should attract government support according to clearly defined rules. This might take the form of direct grants to the company, tax relief or support for research at partner institutes. Such strategies might be voluntary for private companies but if they pass the same appraisal test they should be eligible for the same government support. If companies lack the ability to draw up such strategies, the help could be made available from outside (consultants, higher education institutes, *etc*).

Such an approach could improve networking between institutes and enterprises, build up the capacity of enterprises to undertake R&D and innovate successfully, and build local, regional or sectoral innovation systems. Where different companies identify similar areas of technology for development, these plans could help form the basis of new collaborative public-private R&D programmes involving several firms and universities/ RAS institutes along the lines of the Megaprojects (see below). Participation of foreign firms should, subject to safeguards, be regarded as a bonus.

Public-private partnerships (P/PPs)

PP/Ps are both the desired outcome of effective industry-science relationships and the best catalytic measure that could be envisaged to ensure such effectiveness, based on OECD countries' experience,[8]. They take a variety of different forms and can be used to address a number of different policy issues,[9] but their major contribution is in developing the infrastructure for knowledge and technology diffusion and in supporting collaboration between private firms and PROs to undertake R&D.

Existing P/PPs

P/PPs are not unknown in Russia but their policy frameworks, and their number, size, technological scope and geographical spread are very limited. This is due in large part to the lack industry motivation, but this also reflects to some extent misunderstandings (or false expectations) within the public research sector as to what P/PPs are about. They are too often seen as merely a financing instrument by which researchers could attract additional funding without altering their research agenda. There is thus room for both improvement of existing schemes and new initiatives that would contribute more decisively to increase the breadth, depth and economic relevance of the national R&D portfolio.

In 2003, six pilot Technology Transfer Centres (TTCs), one in each of six federal districts, were created. Applications from a variety of public organisations were invited with the six winners receiving a government contract to establish a TTC to carry out the following functions:

8. They represent a growing and already sizeable share of total S&T budgets (*e.g.* more than 6% in the Netherlands) and now, often the bulk of competitive funding for technological development (*e.g.* almost 80% of competitive grants financed through the Funds for Technological Research of the French Ministry of Research).

9. These include funding early-stage technology development; providing a means by which universities, PROs and private research contractors can be funded to help companies (usually SMEs) to upgrade their technological competences and receive expert advice; fostering the development of technical standards and developing the technologies needed for innovation friendly regulation; enhancing the capacity for innovation and economic competitiveness of individual regions or local areas and the development of high-technology geographical clusters; enabling innovation in goods and services purchased by public sector bodies; and promoting the development of technologies, products and services to meet the needs of the public sector and social needs more generally.

- Selection and appraisal of commercially promising projects.
- Provision of help and advice on the protection of intellectual property including patents, copyrights, trademarks, etc., and on patent searches.
- Help and advise on the drafting of licensing agreements, engineering consulting services contracts and RTD and industrial collaboration agreements.
- Assessment of the contribution of the various intellectual inputs to joint ventures.
- Provision of legal assistance in cases of IPR infringement and unfair competition.
- Assistance with the management of new firms created to commercialised R&D outputs.

Each TTC was provided with RUB 3 million, which had to be matched by other sources (federal ministries and departments, local budgets, own resources, private sector). Promises of private sector funding were greatly weighted in selecting successful applicants. As a pilot programme, its results will have to be evaluated rigorously with a view to deciding whether there should be future implementation on a larger scale. One question which would already deserve more careful consideration is whether TTCs are intended to complement or compete with smaller intermediary structures that have proliferated from bottom-up and unco-ordinated initiatives.

As regards collaborative R&D, the Russian government took an important initiative in 2002 by launching a set of 12 *"Megaprojects"*. This programme is the first real attempt to mobilise the expertise of the public research sector to help Russian industry improve its competitiveness on both home and foreign markets in areas of strategic importance (see Table A1.5 in Annex 1 for the main features of the programme compared to those of selected OECD country P/PP programmes, as well as a brief description of each Megaproject in Annex 2). Each megaproject aims to complete a whole innovation cycle of applied research, development, utilisation and market launch in 3-4 years, including clearly defined sales targets of at least five times the funds provided from the state budget. Both research institutes and commercial firms are involved with the former, acting as the main contractor in a majority of the projects. R&D and engineering development costs are met from the federal budget with manufacturing and other downstream costs being met by the firms involved. The total cost of the programme is budgeted at RUB 8 billion, of which half will be met from the federal budget. The 12 projects were selected from a much larger number and successful applicants received a government contract.

The megaprojects typically involve the design and experimental testing of a number of different product prototypes, engineering development of the preferred design, development of an appropriate method of serial manufacture, and resulting product launch. One objective is to overcome the attitude of industrial organisations inherited from the Soviet era that the services of the research (and innovation!) sector could be taken for granted. Systematic monitoring of the set-up phase of the projects was implemented for the first time in Russia.

It is clearly too early to judge the technical and commercial impacts of the programme. The first consistent pieces of evidence would not have been visible before the end of 2004, and an interim assessment of the effectiveness of the programme as a whole will not be possible before 2006. This evaluation will be necessary to decide whether a second round of calls for proposals (including propositions to extend current projects) should be envisaged and, in the affirmative, how any fine-tuning of the progamme could be warranted.

This evaluation will have to cope with the large variety of megaprojects in terms of size, strategic importance for the country, and potential for success. It will have also to judge retrospectively the merit of an approach which aims to enhance innovation capabilities of industry by supporting near-market technological development in narrowly-defined fields (see Table A1.5 in Annex 1), compared to other PP/P approaches (Table 3.3). Among the questions which will have to be answered, four of the most important are: Would supported projects have been implemented without government support? Do research outcomes have the best chances of commercialisation without stronger involvement of major end users or changes in some framework conditions (*e.g.* more environment-friendly regulation)? What failure rate is acceptable for applied, close-to-market research? How to deal with situations where technical and commercial success is likely, but at a cost far above what was initially expected?

A second P/PP model that has been implemented in Russia is the interdepartmental innovation programme "*Biotechnology for Medicine and Agriculture*" introduced in 2001. This is a priority technology area for Russia and it was felt that federal budget support for this technology "cluster" was not sufficient to bring the research outputs to the market. The programme funds pre-competitive R&D and commercialisation of the resulting outputs via a mixture of public funding and finance from private commercial organisations, from the development of technical specifications to production of competitive, high-level biotechnology products.

Table 3.3. **A typology of P/PPs with Russian and foreign examples***

		Type of industrial activity to which PROs contribute through the PP/P		
		Technological development	Applied research	Pre-competitive research
Type of end users	Mission-oriented	• A few ***Megaprojects***	• Some Australian "national benefits" CRCs • Some projects in some French RRITs	• Some ***"Biotechnology for Medicine and Agriculture"*** projects • Some Australian "national benefits" CRCs • Some French RRITs
	Market-oriented	• Most ***Megaprojects***	• A few ***Megaprojects*** • Some ***"Biotechnology for Medicine and Agriculture"*** projects • Australian "Business Development" CRCs • Most Austrian Kind/Knet	• Most ***"Biotechnology for Medicine and Agriculture"*** *projects* • Australian "Industrial collaboration" CRCs • Most Austrian Kplus • Most French RRITs • Dutch LTIs

* CRCs = Co-operative Research Centres; Kind/Knet and Kplus = Competence Centres; LTIs = Leading Technology Institutes; RRITs = National Networks for Technological Innovation.

The programme has already brought together about 300 biotechnology projects undertaken by academic institutes, research and industrial organisations. Forms of collaboration are diverse. In some cases, commercial development of the most significant and promising R&D has required the creation of new research and commercial organisations which will bring research results to the production stage. The programme is open to both national and international participants.

The programme is administered by an interdepartmental co-ordination council composed of scientists, entrepreneurs and investors, company representatives, and federal executive bodies. Routine management is provided by an executive board which reports to the Council. In order to encourage investment in the programme, participants have established a non-profit partnership, the "Biotechnological Consortium on Medicine and Agriculture (BIOMAC)". Consortium members include principal Russian manufacturers of biotechnology products and financiers (including joint-stock companies).

The Consortium's objective is to muster various types of non-budget finance (venture financing, direct investment, credit on favourable terms) to support science-intensive innovation ventures. The programme creates a common information space for researchers and developers, manufacturers and investors. It facilitates access to state support for those undertaking R&D in priority fields, enables investors to finance highly profitable high-technology production, and allows manufacturers to launch competitive, high value-added products.

Finally, throughout the vast Russian innovation system there are a myriad of bottom-up P/PP initiatives to achieve very diverse goals. Many popped up without any government intervention. One example is the two-year agreement reached in 2003 between Norilsk Nikel and the Russian Academy of Sciences on co-operation in the field of hydrogen power.[10] This is a sign of vitality in the system which should not be suppressed by any inadequate attempt by the government to impose rigid models for partnerships. Bottom-up initiatives should rather be "disciplined by rewarding" the best and consolidated by a catalytic programme to create synergies in specific fields.

10. During the first stage of this cooperation the RAS will receive USD 40 million per year for R&D to be carried out in 20 of its institutes.

Table 3.4. **Comparative size of programmes in Russia and selected OECD countries**

Annual budget expenditures, EUR millions

Type of programme		Name of programme	Budget
Promotion of networking between higher education, other PROs and industry through small research grants	Russia	Education-Research Centres	5
	Australia	ARC Linkage Grants & Fellowships	45
	Austria	Christian Doppler Laboratories	4
	Netherlands	STW Technology Foundation	43
PP/Ps to promote collaborative R&D between PROs and industry	Russia	Megaprojects	30
	Australia	CRCs	88
	Austria	Kind/Knet and Kplus	36
	France	RRITs	174
	Netherlands	LTIs	29
	United States	ATP	100

Source: OECD.

The need for new governmental initiatives

The successful launch of the Megaprojects and the Biotechnology Research Consortium demonstrates that the basic conditions, including the legal framework, for the operation of P/PPs exists in Russia, even if they could be improved. But the existing P/PP programmes are still of a very modest scale and scope considering the dimension of the Russian economy that they are intended to dynamise (Table 3.4). The main obstacles to further use of P/PPs as a key tool in Russian innovation policy are:

- The attitude of the part of industry that has been accustomed for too long to seeing PROs as either irrelevant to their business or only a cheap source of technological services.
- The symmetrical mind-set in PROs, which sees industry as mostly a source of funding and not as a partner in ambitious research ventures.
- The lack of broad-based political will. Here, the government can make the difference with targeted actions which, through a demonstration effect, could trigger cascading positive changes.

There is therefore a strong need as well as opportunities to create types of P/PPs not yet deployed in Russia, following international best practices. Concrete suggestions were presented in the first part of this report.

Conclusion

Russia faces the challenge of economic diversification through the accelerated development of innovation-driven activities. Based on an analysis of the strengths and weaknesses of its innovation system, this report has identified industry-science relationships as the area where government could have greater leverage in its effort to promote innovation. Public-private partnership is the key policy instrument to better connect science to innovation while catalysing a cascade of positive changes throughout the Russian innovation system. There is still great and untapped potential for the development of P/PPs that new government initiatives could help realise.

Annex 1

COMPLEMENTARY STATISTICS AND INFORMATION

Table A1.1. **Revealed comparative advantage (RCA)**

		RCA			Export share	
33	Petroleum, petroleum products and related materials	23.8	31.7	38.9	40.4	40.4
34	Gas, natural and manufactured	18.3	15.3	13.7	14.0	54.4
93	Special transactions and commodities not classified	-14.7	-22.9	7.9	8.5	62.8
68	Non-ferrous metals	8.3	6.9	5.2	6.0	68.8
67	Iron and steel	5.7	2.8	3.0	6.5	75.3
24	Cork and wood	2.0	2.0	2.4	2.4	77.7
56	Fertilizers	1.8	1.5	1.5	1.6	79.3
32	Coal, coke and briquettes	0.7	0.9	1.1	1.6	80.8
79	Other transport equipment	-1.3	0.6	1.1	2.8	83.7
25	Pulp and waste paper	0.4	0.5	0.4	0.5	84.2
51	Organic chemicals	0.7	0.6	0.4	1.2	85.4
23	Crude rubber (including synthetic and reclaimed)	0.4	0.2	0.3	0.4	85.8
35	Electric current	0.6	0.1	0.2	0.3	86.1
04	Cereals and cereal preparations	-1.4	-1.5	0.1	1.0	87.1
61	Leather, leather manufactures and dressed fur skins	0.0	0.0	0.1	0.1	87.2
21	Hides, skins and fur skins, raw	0.4	0.1	0.04	0.1	87.3
71	Power-generating machinery and equipment	0.0	0.3	0.03	1.5	88.8

Source: United Nations, Commodity Trade Statistics Database (COMTRADE).

Figure A1.1. **Productivity: levels and changes in the 30 most important industrial sectors**

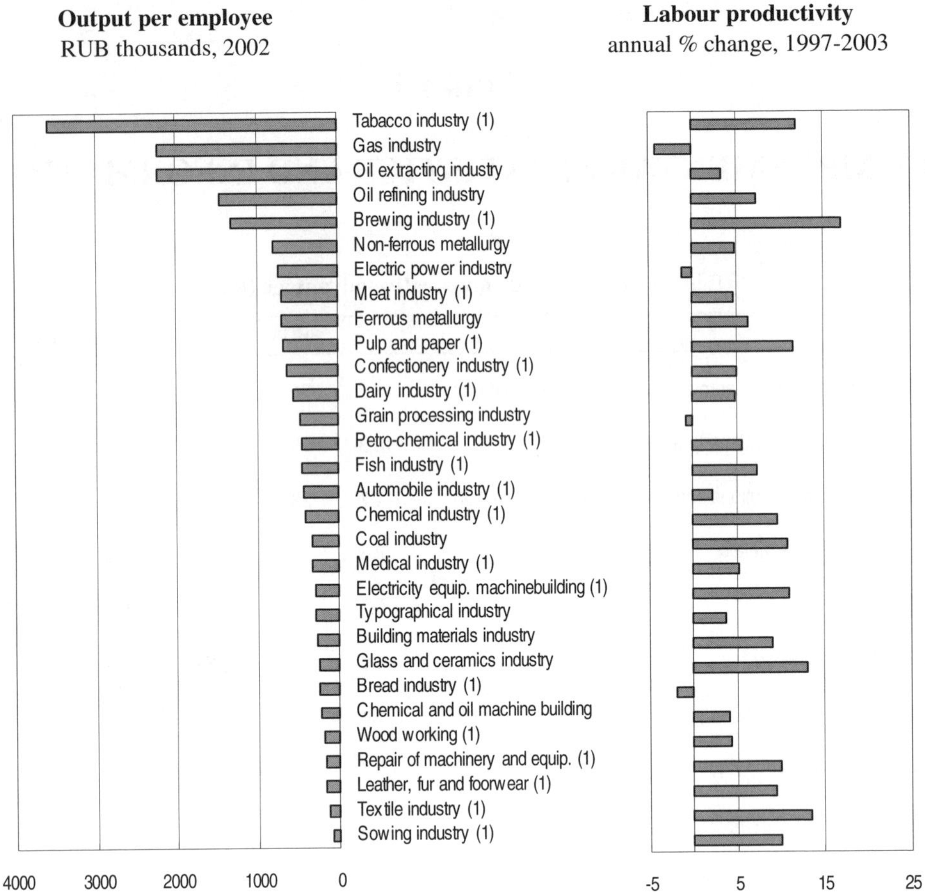

1. Data for 1997-2002.

Source: Reproduced from the 2004 OECD Economic Survey of the Russian Federation.

Figure A1.2. **The Russian Innovation System**

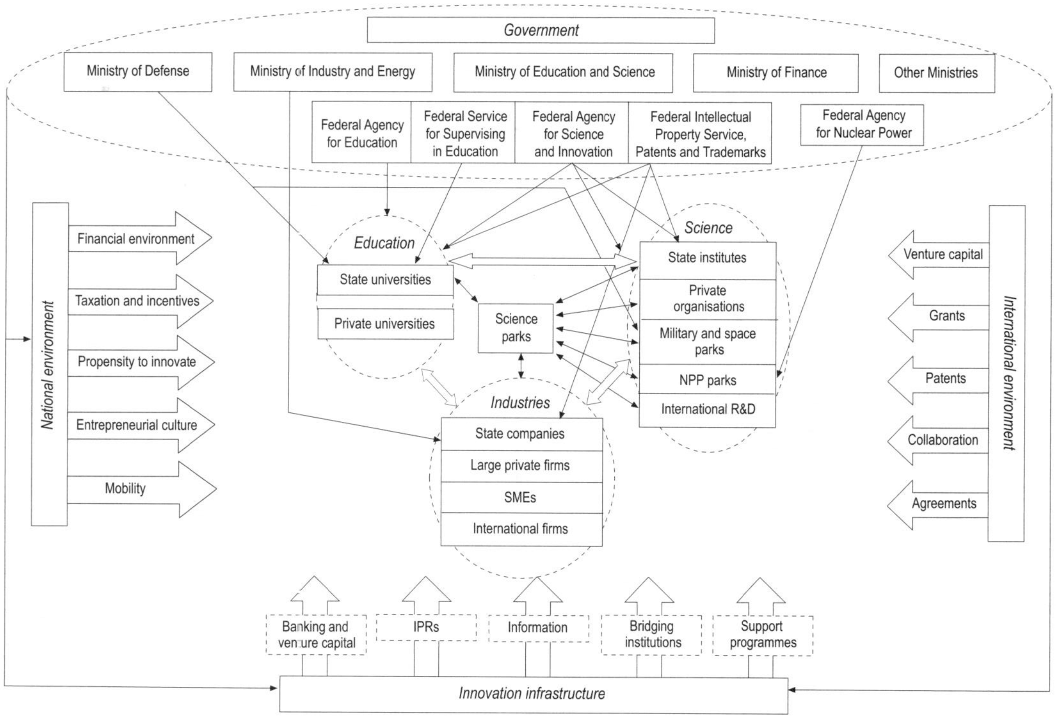

Table A1.2. **Ownership of the Russian R&D Sector**

Percentage of total number of research organisations, 2002

Public	71
Private	12
Mixed	14
Foreign and joint Russian-foreign	2
Other	1

Source: Goskomstat.

Table A1.3. **R&D intensity of Russia's federal districts and ten leading regions**

Percentage, 1998-2001

	1998	2000	2002
Central FD	1.57	1.59	1.85
- Moscow Region	3.05	3.72	3.39
- Kaluga Region	2.06	2.24	3.10
- Moscow	1.71	1.62	2.00
- Voronezh Region	1.18	1.42	1.39
Northwest FD	1.31	1.47	1.65
- St. Petersburg	2.86	3.65	3.40
- Leningrad Region	1.31	1.21	1.57
Volga FD	0.89	1.02	1.27
- Nizhny Novgorod R.	2.89	3.81	4.05
- Ulianovsk Region	1.90	2.35	2.52
- Samara Region	0,96	1,52	1,85
Siberia FD	0,52	0,57	0,73
- Novosibirsk Region	1,88	2,19	2,25
South FD	0,44	0,49	0,53
Fareast FD	0,32	0,45	0,53
Ural FD	0,43	0,29	0,32
Russian Federation	*0,95*	*1,05*	*1,24*

Source: Russian Ministry of Education and Science.

Table A1.4. **Geographical dispersion of Russia's research and innovation activities**

Percentage, 2002

	1	2	3	4	5	6	7	8	9	10	Total
Patent applications	23.2	8.0	7.1	8.2	2.7	2.2	2.3	2.4	2.6	2.3	23 712
Patents granted	*22.8*	*6.8*	*8.4*	*3.0*	*2.7*	*2.5*	*2.6*	*2.7*	*3.2*	*2.7*	*15 140*
R&D expenses	34.9	10.4	11.0	1.1	1.3	6.6	1.5	3.4	2.9	2.4	4 091
- Basic research	*38.2*	*7.9*	*10.2*	*1.2*	*0.9*	*1.5*	*0.7*	*0.3*	*2.6*	*8.1*	599
- Applied research	*34.0*	*11.1*	*9.9*	*3.3*	*0.8*	*11.1*	*0.6*	*0.6*	*1.4*	*2.8*	652
- Product development	*34.5*	*10.7*	*11.3*	*0.6*	*1.6*	*6.6*	*1.9*	*4.7*	*3.3*	*1.1*	2 842
Innovative organisations	5.6	4.7	3.9	1.0	4.2	3.4	2.1	3.4	5.1	1.3	2 498
Research staff	31.4	10.4	10.8	1.0	1.8	5.5	1.5	2.9	3.1	2.9	870 878
- Doctors	*49.6*	*6.9*	*12.4*	*0.8*	*1.2*	*1.7*	*0.5*	*0.6*	*2.2*	*5.9*	*22 571*
- Candidates	*44.6*	*8.1*	*12.5*	*0.9*	*1.5*	*2.1*	*0.6*	*0.7*	*2.3*	*4.7*	*79 775*

1 = Moscow. 2 = Moscow region. 3 = St. Petersburg. 4 = Krasnodar region. 5 = Republic of Tatarstan.
6 = Nizhny Novgorod region. 7 = Perm region. 8 = Samara region. 9 = Sverdlovsk region. 10 = Novosibirsk region.

Source: Russian Ministry of Education and Science.

Box A1.1. **The role of networking and intellectual property rights in a knowledge economy**

Networking

The increasing importance of industry-science relationships is only one aspect of the way in which the whole innovation system, indeed the whole economy, is becoming more networked. Successful innovation increasingly depends on an open approach in which firms leverage both internal and external sources of ideas and capabilities. Suppliers of materials, components, software and services are increasingly required to play a significant and proactive role in the innovation efforts of their customers. Firms are reducing their dependence on central research laboratories (where these still exist) and commissioning research from universities and public and private research laboratories.

In some sectors the development of new leading-edge technologies is being left to SMEs, which will often license their discoveries to large firms or be taken over by the latter. Collaborative research undertaken by two or more companies is now much more common, often involving universities and PROs as well. Distributed innovation where co-ordinated innovations in complementary goods and services are undertaken by consortia of firms is increasingly recognised. Complex products or engineering systems which are constructed jointly by consortia of firms appear to account for about one-fifth of industrial production.

Firms that wish to innovate successfully must be able to access appropriate science, technology and business competences from wherever they are to be found. This requires firms to develop, maintain, manage and effectively exploit often quite extensive external networks.

Intellectual property rights (IPRs)

In OECD countries, these developments are being accompanied by much greater emphasis placed by both by business firms and the public research sector on discoveries protected by IPR. Firms need to investigate a much wider range of technologies than in the past and are more likely to make inventions which are not immediately relevant to their business. In a world in which more and more firms are searching for external sources of technology, it pays to protect these inventions by good quality (well-researched) IPRs. Income from licensing is increasingly seen as making a significant contribution to total profits. In these circumstances individual firms must be careful to protect the technologies they develop to further their core businesses with IPR which will stand up in international courts. There is an increasing risk that one firm will unknowingly infringe intellectual property claimed by another and without good quality IPR, it will not be in a position to either defend itself legally or negotiate.

Box A1.1. **The role of networking and intellectual property rights in a knowledge economy *(continued)***

Governments are now much more concerned about patenting the results of publicly funded R&D in order to:

- Recoup all or part of the public funds expended from profits resulting from subsequent commercial exploitation.
- Provide an incentive for public researchers and research institutions to undertake commercially promising research.
- Facilitate the transfer of the results of that research to the business sector.

Apart from a limited number of successful research institutions (mainly in the United States) this emphasis on patenting the results of publicly funded research has yet to achieve the success that was hoped for. Results of academic research are often at a very early stage in the development of a new technology and their commercial value is often hard to assess. In some cases commercial exploitation depends on the development of complementary technologies. Those negotiating the licensing of IPRs on behalf of universities and research institutes are often new to this activity, inexperienced and inclined to claim that IPR is worth more than a prudent firm will be prepared to pay. Pressure from university authorities and institute directors may encourage them to make these claims. There are now frequent stories of firms walking away from negotiations with universities over IPR-related matters or even refusing to enter into negotiations at all. It appears that most universities in the United States and United Kingdom have so far failed to earn enough income from licensing the results of research to cover the costs involved, although there are a few notable exceptions. Of course, the closer the results of research to exploitation, the easier it will be to define and value the intellectual property involved.

Given that the main objective should be to ensure that the results of publicly funded research should be exploited for the benefit of the country concerned, patenting of such results may not always be the best option. Often a firm may require an exclusive licence whereas the national interest may require wider diffusion to a number of firms. Scientific and technological knowledge is a public good which can be used by many firms and people without one firms use excluding that of another. The whole scientific endeavour, and the long-term economic and social benefits which it yields, depends on the ready availability of research findings to the rest of the research community for use in further research.

Table A1.5. **Comparative features of PP/P programmes in Russia and selected OECD countries**

	CRCs (Australia)	Kplus, Kind/Knet (Austria)	RRITs (France)	LTIs (Netherlands)	Megaprojects (Russia)
Duration					
Starting	1990	Kplus: 1998; Kind/Knet: 1999	1999	1997	2002
Period	7 years	4 years with the possibility of extension for another 3 years.	Open	4 years	3-4 years
Coverage					
Number of centres (networks)	96 centres since inception, of which 70 are currently operating	18 Kplus centres 17 Kind/Knet centres/networks	16 networks	4 centres	12 projects
Research fields	Very varied	Very varied	Very varied	Focus on four areas (polymers, telecommunications, food sciences, metals technology)	Narrowly defined areas, mainly in manufacturing
Participants					
Selection process	Competitive – 15 out of the first 120 applications in 1991 Evaluation by: two external technical expert advisory panels; national and international referees; the CRC Committee	Competitive Assessed through an independent, international peer review	Competitive The selection of projects involves two phases: preparation and calls for proposals; and scientific expertise and project certification	Competitive – 4 out of 19 initial proposals Evaluation by external group of experts	Competitive The Competition authorities were involved in setting the procedures. Evaluation by an Expert Council, based on the opinion of a number of independent experts, and list of priority technological fields drawn by the Ministry
Participants per centre	15 organisations on average, of which universities (40%), firms (32%), public labs (24%)	Require participation of at least a public research organisation and five firms	On average firms get 46% of public funding, compared to 36% for public labs and 20% for universities	20 companies and 8 public research organisations, on average	Not many, under the leadership of an "executive organisation" (an industrial firm or a PRO)
Participation of SMEs	Enhancing the participation of SMEs has become a higher priority in the latest selection round	Kplus: about 25% of the industrial partners are SMEs Kind/Knet: technological needs of SMEs are among the eligibility criteria	Ensuring that SMEs participate in or benefit from co-operative research is an important objective of all RRITs SMEs get at least 20% of the budget appropriations	No specific incentives The share of SMEs is limited (10%), partly owing to the research focus of LTIs	No specific incentives The share of SMEs is very limited, reflecting the Russian industrial structure in the selected technological areas

Table A1.5. **Comparative features of PP/P programmes in Russia and selected OECD countries** *(continued)*

	CRCs (Australia)	Kplus, Kind/Knet (Austria)	RRITs (France)	LTIs (Netherlands)	Megaprojects (Russia)
Participation of foreign companies	Collaboration within international research networks is an explicit selection criterion.	Foreign firms can fully take part in a Kplus centre. Participation in international programmes is included among evaluation criteria Out of 285 industrial partners participating in Kplus centres, 36 (*i.e.* 13%) are foreign	Foreign domiciled firms are allowed to participate in all RRITs	Non-domiciled firms, as well as foreign public research organisations, can participate, subject to government approval Foreign researchers account for 21% of LTIs workforce	Participation seems to be allowed, at own expenses, but does not seem significant so far
Financing					
Cost-sharing	Two thirds of all resources are provided by the CRC programme, universities, CSIRO and other Commonwealth organisations. Only one-quarter of the resources are provided by industry and other non-government sources	Up to 35% federal funds, a maximum 25% from other public sources, and a minimum 40% from industry	Industry participation ranges from almost one-half to around one-third. Public research represent from 27% of the budget appropriations for space and aeronautics to 42% in life sciences Participation of universities is very diverse: from 5% in life sciences to 19% in ICTs	Government funding: at most 50% Public research organisations: at least 20% Firms: at least 20%	Government funding: at most 50%
Self-sustainability	Self-sustainability is an objective but there are very few examples of CRCs reaching such stage	Self-sustainability is an objective	Self-sustainability is not an explicit objective	By the end of 2007, LTIs should be self-sustained	Self-sustainability is not an explicit objective There are strict deadlines for the completion of projects
Organisation					
Organisational form (central or virtual)	Participants have considerable freedom to choose the arrangement they consider to be most appropriate	Most Kplus centres operate at one physical location Most Kind/Knet are virtual centres	RRITs are virtual networks made up of companies, laboratories, experts and representatives of government	Some are purely virtual, others have a mixed organisational form	Most of the work is done at the site of the "executive agency"
Legal status	Mostly unincorporated joint ventures, but incorporation is encouraged	Incorporated (limited companies)	Special status (GIE)	Incorporated (limited companies)	Special status

Table A1.5. **Comparative features of PP/P programmes in Russia and selected OECD countries** *(continued)*

	CRCs (Australia)	Kplus, Kind/Knet (Austria)	RRITs (France)	LTIs (Netherlands)	Megaprojects (Russia)
Intellectual Property Rights	No general rules for all centres The government does not claim any share in the IPRs generated by CRCs IPRs developed in the course of the research by a CRC belong to the CRC and in the case of CRCs which are not legal entities in their own right (*i.e.* unincorporated joint ventures) the IPRs are held by one of the public-sector partners on behalf of the CRC participants	Kplus: • Basic research: all IPRs belong to the centre and each partner has the right to use the results • Industrial research with partner companies: all IPRs belong to the centre and each partner of the project has the right to use the results. Kind/Knet: IPR issues are addressed on an *ad hoc* basis	RRITs have a minimal IPR policy, which consists of ensuring that all IPR issues are covered by an agreement between all those involved in a joint R&D project For a project to be eligible, all actors must approve a prior draft IPR agreement But the actual details of the apportioning of IPRs among the various categories of actors, both private and public, are ad hoc arrangements between the parties and not subject to any specific policy or guidelines.	No explicit requirements about IPR allocation among partners – IPR issues are addressed on an *ad hoc* basis	In order to facilitate contractual arrangements between participants, special contracts were concluded for every individual projects, in which the ownership of existing and future IP is clearly defined
Evaluation	Each centre is formally evaluated after one, two and five years The CRC programme as a whole underwent external reviews in 1995, 1997 and 2003	Kplus have been so far subject to a more rigorous evaluation process than Kind/Knet: • An *ex ante* evaluation • After a first term of four years, *interim* evaluation An *ex post* evaluation after seven years	The evaluation of research project proposals (project achievements) or the internal or external audit of operations, which are core tasks or good management practices of the RRITs	Extensive formal evaluation every four years	A strict monitoring process is implemented Very precise technical and commercialisation targets have been defined from the start

Table A1.6. **List of co-operative research centres (networks) currently operating, classified by technological field**

Australia (CRCs)	**Austria** (Kplus and Kind/Knet)	**France** (RRITs)	**Netherlands** (LTIs)	**Russia** (Megaprojects)
		Manufacturing technologies		
Advanced composite structures	Mechatronics	Earth and space	Polymers	Sealing and fire-protection materials
Bioproducts	Applied biocatalysis	Aeronautics	Metals	Instruments and equipment for nanotechnologies
CAST metals manufacturing	Tribology	Land transport		Electronic modules (PEM) for infra-red equipment
Intelligent manufacturing technologies	Tech research	Urban planning and civil works		Catalytic technologies for the production of motor fuels
Microtechnology	Applied electrochemistry	Materials and processes		High quality cardboard with the use of secondary fibres
Polymers	Light metals	Nanotechnology		Structural metallic materials
Welded structures	Materials			New generation of synthetic crystals
Construction innovation	Polymers			More efficient and environment-friendly diesel engines
Functional communication surfaces	Wood composites & chemistry			
Innovative wood manufacturing	Industrial mathematics			
Railway engineering and technologies	Materials and engineering for aeronautics			
	Wood construction			
	Wood technology			
	Wood research			
	Acoustic			
	Automation			
	Light technologies			
		Information and communication technologies		
Satellite systems	Advanced computer vision	Earth and space	Telematics	
Photonics	Telecommunications	Land transport		
Telecommunications	Knowledge management	Telecommunications		
Distributed systems technology	Software	Nanotechnology		
Sensor signal and information processing	Virtual reality	Software		

Table A1.6. **List of co-operative research centres (networks) currently operating, classified by technological field** *(continued)*

Australia (CRCs)	**Austria** (Kplus and Kind/Knet)	**France** (RRITs)	**Netherlands** (LTIs)	**Russia** (Megaprojects)
Smart internet technology	Electronic commerce	Multimedia		
Technology enabled capital markets	Interactive e-business			
		Mining and energy		
Greenhouse gas technology	Bioenergy	Fuel cells		Steam gas power installations
Mining technology and equipment	Renewable energy			More efficient production of heat
Hydrometallurgy				
Clean power from lignite				
Coal in sustainable development				
Landscape environments and mineral exploration				
Predictive mineral discovery				
		Agriculture and rural-based manufacturing		
Sustainable sugar production		Génoplante	Food	Seed material for genetically modified agricultural plants
Molecular plant breeding				
Sustainable forestry production				
Sustainable rice production				
Cotton				
Cattle and beef quality				
Tropical plant protection				
Viticulture				
Sheep industry				
Innovative dairy products				
Sustainable aquaculture of finfish				
Innovative grain food products				

Table A1.6. **List of co-operative research centres (networks) currently operating, classified by technological field** *(continued)*

Australia (CRCs)	**Austria** (Kplus and Kind/Knet)	**France** (RRITs)	**Netherlands** (LTIs)	**Russia** (Megaprojects)
		Environment		
Antarctica and the Southern Ocean	Natural hazard management	Earth and space		More efficient and environment-friendly diesel engines
Sustainable tourism	Recycling product development	Land transport		Improved treatment of solid wastes
Environmental biotechnology	Environment-friendly engines	Water and environment technology		
Biological control of pest animals	Environment techrology processes	Maritime accidental pollutions		
Catchment hydrology		Urban planning and civil works		
Coastal zone, estuary and waterway management				
Freshwater ecology				
The Great Barrier Reef World Heritage area				
Greenhouse accounting				
Tropical rainforest ecology and management				
Weed management				
Plant-based management of dryland salinity				
Tropical savannas management				
Water quality and treatment				
		Medical science and technology		
Aboriginal and tropical health	Bio-molecular therapeutics	Genhomme		
Cellular growth factors	Biopharmaceutical technology	Nanotechnology		
Discovery of genes for common human diseases	Medicine	Health technologies		
Eye Research and Technology	Health information technologies			
Vaccine technology				
Asthma				
Chronic inflammatory diseases				
Cochlear implant and hearing aid innovation				
Diagnostics				

Annex 2

LIST OF "MEGAPROJECTS"

PROJECT 1: Developing a new generation of sealing and fire-protection materials with wide industrial application

Executing agency: CJSC Unichimtech, Moscow.

Budget funding: RUB 400 million, including RUB 140 million in 2003.

Extra budgetary resources: RUB 410.2 million, including RUB 140.2 million in 2003.

Expected sales volume: RUB 3 500 million by 2007.

PROJECT 2: Developing and mastering the production of instruments and equipment for nanotechnologies

Executing agency: CJSC NT-MTD, Moscow.

Budget funding: RUB 400 million, including RUB 120 million in 2003.

Extra budgetary resources: RUB 410.5 million, including RUB 70.5 million in 2003.

Expected sales volume: RUB 2 300 million by 2007, starting from 2005.

PROJECT 3: Biotechnological development and production of seeds of genetically modified agricultural plants

Executing agency: GU Bioengineering Centre, RAS, Moscow.

Budget funding: RUB 150 million, including RUB 80 million in 2003.

Extra budgetary resources: RUB 170 million in total, including RUB 50 million in 2003.

Expected sales volume by 2008: Sugar beet seeds (not less than 400 tonnes and RUB 140 million per year); potato seeds (not less than 80 000 tonnes and RUB 1 billion per year).

PROJECT 4: Developing and mastering the production of photo-electronic modules (PEM) for infra-red equipment

Executing agency: FGUP, Orion Scientific and Production Association, Moscow.

Budget funding: RUB 300 million in total, including in RUB 120 million in 2003.

Extra budgetary resources: RUB 150 million in total, including RUB 15 million in 2003.

Expected sales volume: RUB 3 000 million by 2008, starting from 2005.

PROJECT 5: Developing and mastering the production of a new generation of catalysts and catalytic technologies for the production of motor fuels

Executing agency: Institute of Catalysis, Siberian Department of RAS, Novosibirsk.

Budget funding: RUB 350 million, including RUB 250 million in 2003.

Extra budgetary resources: RUB 653 million, including RUB 22 million in 2003.

Expected sales volume: Not less than RUB 600 million per year.

PROJECT 6: Developing and mastering the production of new types of high-quality cardboard

Executing agency: OJSC Central Scientific Research Institute of Paper, Pravdinsky settlement, Moscow region.

Budget financing: RUB 150 million, including RUB 60 million in 2003.

Extra budgetary resources: RUB 318.7 million, including RUB 21.3 million in 2003.

Expected sales volume: Not less than RUB 2 000 million by 2008, starting from 2005.

PROJECT 7: Developing and mastering the production of highly effective steam gas power installations of more than 200 megawatts

Executing agency: OJSC Lenigradsky Metallic Plant, St. Petersburg.

Budget financing: RUB 450 million, including RUB 150 million in 2003.

Extra budgetary resources: RUB 550 million, including RUB 199.5 million in 2003.

Expected sales volume: Not less than RUB 2 500 million by 2007, starting from 2004.

PROJECT 8: Developing and mastering the production of structural metallic materials with a two-fold increase of the most important operational properties

Executing agency: FGUP Prometheus Central Scientific Research Institute of Structural Materials, St. Petersburg.

Budget funding: RUB 200 million, including RUB 60 million in 2003.

Extra budgetary resources: RUB 200 million, including RUB 26 million in 2003.

Expected sales volume: RUB 1 000 million by 2007, starting from 2005.

PROJECT 9: Development of synthetic crystal dielectrics and related articles

Executing agency: GU Institute of Crystallography, Moscow.

Budget funding: RUB 460 million, including RUB 100 million in 2003.

Extra budgetary resources: RUB 501 million, including RUB 10 million in 2003.

Expected sales volume: RUB 2 300 million by 2006.

PROJECT 10: Developing and mastering the production of competitive diesel engines for automobile and other purposes

Executing agency: OJSC Zavolzhsky motor plant, town of Zavolzhie 2, Nizhegordskaya area.

Budget financing: RUB 500 million, including RUB 105 million in 2003.

Extra budgetary resources: RUB 2 041 million, including RUB 300 million in 2003.

Expected sales volume: RUB 4 000 million per year, starting from 2006.

PROJECT 11: Development and fine-tuning of technical, technological, organisational and financial solutions to improve the efficiency of the heating supply in Russia

Executing agency: OJSC Fuel Investment Company of the City of Syktyvkar, Republic of Komi, Syktyvkar.

Budget funding: RUB 250 million, including RUB 40 million in 2003.

Extra budgetary resources: RUB 1 800 million, including RUB 40 million in 2003.

Target: Reduction of heating supply expenditures by 40%.

PROJECT 12: Raising the effectiveness of solid waste processing

Executing agency: OJSC "Mechanobr-technika", St. Petersburg.

Budget funding: RUB 400 million, including RUB 40 million in 2003.

Extra budgetary resources: RUB 427.5 million in total, including RUB 28 million in 2003.

Expected sales volume: RUB 2 250 million by 2006.

Annex 3

INTERNATIONAL CONFERENCE ON PUBLIC-PRIVATE PARTNERSHIPS FOR INNOVATION: PROGRAMME

Conference co-organised by
The Ministry of Education and Science of the Russian Federation
and the Organisation for Economic Co-operation and Development (OECD)

Le Meridien Moscow Country Club, 16-17 December 2004

The organisers express their deep gratitude to the Federal Service for Intellectual Property, Patents and Trademarks, the Innovation Business Club "Intelcom", the French Embassy in Russia, the "Wimm-Bill-Dann" company, the British Council, Microsoft Russia/CIS and UNDP, whose contributions have made this conference possible. The Donor's Council was co-chaired by David Iakobashvili, Chairman of the Board of Directors, the "Wimm-Bill-Dann" Company, and Gennady Kurapov, Director General, Innovation Business Club "Intelcom."

Conference objectives

- To discuss the role of PP/Ps in an overall strategy to promote innovation-led growth in Russia.
- To present and discuss the draft OECD-Russia PP/Ps project report, especially its part on policy recommendations.
- To disseminate the experience of OECD countries in promoting and managing public-private partnerships for innovation.

Co-Chairs:

- Boris Simonov, Director-General of the Federal Service for Intellectual Property, Patents and Trademarks, Russia
- Daniel Malkin, Head, Science and Technology Policy Division, Directorate for Science, Technology and Industry, OECD

THURSDAY, 16 DECEMBER 2004

9:00 - 9:30	**Registration**
9:30 - 11:00	**Opening session**
9:30 - 10:00	**Welcome addresses** Andrey Fursenko, Minister of Education and Science of the Russian Federation Herwig Schlögl, Deputy Secretary-General, OECD
10:00 - 10:20	**Opening remarks** Philippe Petit, Deputy Director-General, World Intellectual Property Organisation Kristalina Georgieva, Director and Resident Representative in the Russian Federation, World Bank
10:20 - 11:00	**Keynotes speeches: Connecting science to innovation for sustainable growth** *The views of the public sector*, Victor Sadovnichy, Rector, Moscow State University, Russia *A business sector perspective*, Yan Kuhn de Chizelle, Director, Schlumberger Research Laboratory in Moscow
11:00 - 11:15	***Coffee/tea break***
11:15 - 13:15	**Session 1: Public-Private Partnerships for innovation: the experience of OECD countries** *New trends in science and technology policy and the growing importance of PP/Ps*, Jean Guinet, Senior Economist, Science and Technology Policy Division, Directorate for Science, Technology and Industry, OECD **Presentations by OECD countries' representatives** • Alpo Kuparinen, Deputy Director General, Ministry of Trade and Industry, Finland • Michel Ottolander, Senior Policy Adviser, Ministry of Economic Affairs, Netherlands • Fritz Ohler, Managing Director, Technopolis Forschungs – und Beratungs Gesmbh, Austria • Laurent Buisson, Director of Innovation Department , Ministry of Research, France *Q&A and discussion*

13:30 - 14:30	***Lunch***
14:30 - 18:00	**Session 2: The role of PP/Ps in the Russian innovation system**
	Main Features of the Russian Innovation System, Sergey Lavrov, Director General, Economic Analyses Bureau, Russia
	Public-Private Partnerships for Innovation in Russia: The Current State of Play, Natalia Zolotykh, Director General, Transtechnology, Russia
	Improving the Framework Conditions for P/PPs: The Views of the Scientific Community, Sergey Aldoshin, Member of the Presidium of the Russian Academy of Sciences, Russia
	Improving the Framework Conditions for P/PPs: A Business Perspective, Sergey Kravchenko, President, Boeing, Russia/CIS
16:00 - 16:15	***Coffee/tea break***
16:15 - 18:00	**Session 2 *(continued)***
	Learning from Successful Experiments: A Cluster Initiative in St. Petersburg, Grigoriy Itkinson, Director, Svetlana Opto-Electronic, Russia
	Practical Experience in Implementing P/PPs: The Example of a "Megaproject" Managed by the Institute of Crystallography, Michael Kovalchyk, Secretary of the Council for Science, Technology and Education under the President of Russia
	France's Experience in Developing Public-Private Partnership for Innovation with Russia, Alain Gallochat, Counselor for Intellectual Property, Ministry of Research, France
	Q&A and discussion
19:00	***Official reception***

FRIDAY, 17 DECEMBER 2004

9:30 - 10:30	**Session 3: Presentation of the conclusions of the OECD-Russia P/PPs project report**
	Current and Potential Role of P/PPs as an Innovation Policy Tool in Russia, Boris Simonov, Director-General, Federal Service for Intellectual Property, Patents and Trademarks, Russia
	Key Policy Recommendations for Realising this Potential, Daniel Malkin, Head, Science and Technology Policy Division, Directorate for Science, Technology and Industry, OECD
	Q&A and discussion
10:30 - 10:45	***Coffee/tea break***

10:45 - 12:30 **Final panel discussion on policy recommendations**

Co-Chairs: Boris Simonov (Director General, Federal Service for Intellectual Property, Patents and Trademarks, Russia) and Daniel Malkin (Head, Science and Technology Policy Division, OECD

Panelist from Russia:

- Boris Alyeshin, Head, Federal Industry Agency
- Sergey Borisov, President, Opora Russia
- Vitaly Kveder, Director, Institute of Solid State Physics of the Russian Academy of Sciences

Panelists from OECD countries:

- John Barber, Former Chair of the OECD Committee for Scientific and Technological Policy, United Kingdom
- Hannu Hernesniemi, Research Director, Etlatieto, Finland
- Michael Blakeney, Director, Centre for Commercial Law Studies, Queen Mary University of London, United Kingdom
- *Q&A and discussion*
- Summary remarks by co-Chairs

12:30 - 13:30 **Closing ceremony**

12:30 - 13:00 **Sponsors' address**

13:00 - 13:30 **Closing remarks**

- Sergey Borisov, President, Opora Russia, Russia
- Herwig Schlögl, Deputy Secretary-General, OECD
- Andrey Fursenko, Minister of Education and Science, Russia

13:30 - 14:30 ***Official lunch***

14:40 - 15:30 **Press conference**

APPENDIX

List of the persons interviewed during the OECD mission in Russia (4-10 July 2004)[1]

Ministries, federal agencies and foundations

Ministry of Education and Science

- A. Fursenko, Minister for Education and Science
- D. Livanov, Director, Department of Science, Innovation and Intellectual Property
- I. Beliaev, Deputy Director
- A. Naumov, Deputy Director

Ministry of Economic Development and Trade

- M. Gloukhova, Head, Investment Division

Federal Agency for Science and Innovation

- S. Mazurenko, Chief

Federal Agency for Industry

- I. Gorevatski, Deputy Chief

Federal Service for Intellectual Property, Patents and Trademarks

- B. Simonov, Director-General

Foundation for the Assistance to Small Innovative Enterprises

- I. Bortnik, Director-General

1. The OECD review team was composed of Daniel Malkin and Jean Guinet (OECD Science and Policy Division), John Barber (former Chair of the OECD Committee for Scientific and Technological Policy, United Kingdom,), Hernesniemi Hannu (Research Director, Etlatieto, Finland), Juergen Marchat (Programme Director, TIG, Austria) and Natalia Zolotykh (Director, Transtechnology, Russia).

Public research organisations and universities

Russian Academy of Science (RAS)

- S. Aldoshin, member of the RAS Presidium

RAS Institute of Chemical Physics Problems, Chernogolovka

- V. Kveder, Director

Vavilov State Optical Institute, St. Petersburg

- Y. Tsypkin, Deputy Director

Lavochkin Design Bureau

- K. Klefortov, Head of IP Department

International School of Management, St. Petersburg

- A. Yanchevsky, Director and Professor

Institute for the Economy in Transition, Moscow

- I. Dezhina, Leading researcher

State-owned and private firms

Svetlana

- V. Popov, Director-General

Ezan

- V. Borodin, Director

Russian Standard

- I. Kossarev, Director-General

Intermediaries and business associations

Innovation-Technology Centre of the St. Petersburg Regional Foundation for Scientific and Technological Development

- V. Spivak, Director

Technology Transfer Centre of the RAS Institute of Chemical Physics Problems

- V. Troitsky, Director

Technology Transfer Centre "North-West"

- A. Malinovski, General Director
- P. Goulkin, Investment Director

Consortium "Fort Ross"

- V. Makarov, President

Venture Capital

Russian Venture Capital Association

- E. Evdokimov, Project Manager

The Russian Technology Fund

- V. Levitsky, Director

OECD PUBLICATIONS, 2, rue André-Pascal, 75775 PARIS CEDEX 16
PRINTED IN FRANCE
(92 2005 04 1 P) ISBN 92-64-00965-5 – No. 54013 2005